Cyber-Physical Attack Recovery Procedures

A Step-by-Step Preparation and Response Guide

Luis Ayala

Apress®

Cyber-Physical Attack Recovery Procedures: A Step-by-Step Preparation and Response Guide

Luis Ayala
Fredericksburg
Virginia, USA

ISBN-13 (pbk): 978-1-4842-2064-1   ISBN-13 (electronic): 978-1-4842-2065-8
DOI 10.1007/978-1-4842-2065-8

Library of Congress Control Number: 2016943087

Distributed to the book trade worldwide by Springer Science+Business Media New York, 233 Spring Street, 6th Floor, New York, NY 10013. Phone 1-800-SPRINGER, fax (201) 348-4505, e-mail orders-ny@springer-sbm.com, or visit www.springer.com. Apress Media, LLC is a California LLC and the sole member (owner) is Springer Science + Business Media Finance Inc (SSBM Finance Inc). SSBM Finance Inc is a Delaware corporation.

For information on translations, please e-mail rights@apress.com, or visit www.apress.com.

Apress and friends of ED books may be purchased in bulk for academic, corporate, or promotional use. eBook versions and licenses are also available for most titles. For more information, reference our Special Bulk Sales–eBook Licensing web page at www.apress.com/bulk-sales.

Any source code or other supplementary materials referenced by the author in this text is available to readers at www.apress.com. For detailed information about how to locate your book's source code, go to www.apress.com/source-code/.

Printed on acid-free paper

I want to thank my wife, Paula, who has been with me through thick and thin for the last 35 years.

I also thank our son, Christopher.

Contents at a Glance

Contents

About the Author

Luis Ayala worked for the US Department of Defense for more than 25 years, with the past 11 years at the Defense Intelligence Agency. Prior to his appointment as a defense intelligence senior leader in 2008, he held several leadership positions at the branch and division levels.

His tenure culminated with the position as senior technical expert (facilities/construction). Mr. Ayala earned his Bachelor of Architecture degree from Pratt Institute and he received his Master of Science and Technology Intelligence from the National Intelligence University. NIU is the intelligence community's sole accredited, federal degree–granting institution. His master's thesis, titled "Cybersecure Facilities for the Intelligence Community," is classified. Mr. Ayala was awarded the DIA Civilian Expeditionary Medal and the Civilian Combat Support Medal.

About the Technical Reviewer

William Beck has a BS in engineering from the University of South Carolina, majoring in structures and mechanics, and NROTC. He served six years in the US Navy as a lieutenant and naval aviator with a multi- and single engine, land, instrument, and commercial license. After earning an MBA from Webster University in 1980, Mr. Beck was hired by Exxon Co. USA as a subsurface engineer, where he worked his way up to senior engineer and also earned his professional engineer's license in 1985. For 31 years, he worked for the federal government as an engineering branch chief for the General Services Administration's Public Building Service Property Development in Fort Worth, TX.

Mr. Beck is married with two sons and two grandsons. He is an active pilot, scuba diver, traveler, and golfer.

Introduction

You need to accept as fact that eventually your facility will be the target of a cyber-physical attack. The only choice you have in this matter is how your building will be attacked by reducing the number of possible attack vectors. The best you can hope for is a situation where a cyber-physical attack is detected quickly, building equipment automatically shuts down gracefully (before any damage is done or anyone is injured), and building systems can be rapidly restored to normal operation.

This book does not focus on how hackers can get in to your BCS. I don't explain how hackers can overcome firewalls or defeat sophisticated security software. I leave that to others to explain. I don't spend a lot of time discussing how to tell if a cyber-physical attack is underway (when everything shuts down—especially unrelated building systems, you know something's wrong). The objective of this book is to plan how best to respond to a cyber-physical attack so you can make decisions quickly and take proper action to mitigate the impact of the attack. When a cyber-physical attack occurs, the last thing you want to do is make things up as you go. This book advocates a *dynamic attack surface*—automated on-the-fly changes of a building control system's (BCS) characteristics and defensive counter-cyber operations to thwart actions of an adversary.

You can spend millions of dollars beefing up the secure perimeter of a building against a physical attack, but that can all be defeated by a hacker causing equipment already inside the facility to destroy itself or even explode simply by executing a well-planned cyber-physical attack. Having an active and effective malware detection program in place to protect your facilities is great, but it would be meaningless without a well-designed plan that tells building maintenance personnel what to do when a cyber-physical attack is underway.

Cyber-physical attack A classic cyber-physical attack would be when a hacker is able to damage building equipment by sending destructive commands over the BCS to the equipment that changes the configuration setpoints above dangerous levels for which the equipment has not been designed, such as too high pressure or dangerously high temperature. A second type of cyber-physical attack is an attack that does actual physical damage or a coordinated cyber and physical attacks on vulnerable physical systems. For example, in 2013, a sniper shot at and damaged 17 electrical transformers in California, causing them to leak coolant, overheat, and shut down (physical component).[1] The cyber component to this attack was the fact that the attacker also disabled the utility controls system ability to signal an alarm.

---

[1]Smith, Rebecca. "Assault on California Power Station Raises Alarm on Potential for Terrorism" *Wall Street Journal*, February 5, 2014.

Of course, building engineers assume a cyber-physical attack can't happen because of safety devices installed to prevent catastrophic events. It's true that many building control systems have hard-wired safeties designed to shut down equipment and these hard-wired safeties typically are not controlled by the BCS. However, a hacker can use these safety devices as part of the attack—in fact, the hacker is counting on safety devices turning things off. Keep in mind that the Chernobyl nuclear plant also had safety devices that were turned off—by insiders.[2] Sad to say, 40 percent of cyber-attacks are carried out by insiders. In addition, it is not uncommon for insiders to turn off safety features that tend to set off frequent false alarms. The first thing a hacker does after he installs a backdoor is disable safety devices. A second factor to consider is that multiple pieces of equipment will be attacked simultaneously in a well-planned cyber-physical attack. A hacker won't just disable your boilers—he'll disable everything that he can.

Facility engineers rely on equipment alarms to warn when equipment and processes approach dangerous situations and to (hopefully) allow equipment to power down gracefully. Generally, that is the case—unless of course if a hacker changed the configuration setpoints so the building controls "thinks" that a boiler's 322°F water temperature and 1,500 psi pressure in a gas line designed for 400 psi are "normal" setpoints.

Of course, not every equipment failure or power outage is a cyber-physical attack. When your building is attacked, you probably won't suspect it was a hacker—until you see a pattern. Lots of equipment will act "squirrelly" and you'll know—it's a *cyber-physical attack*!

When a cyber-physical attack occurs, it can mean years of court cases, job losses, higher insurance rates, and criminal litigation. Organizations with a high profile in the community have a responsibility to assess the vulnerability of their facilities to disruption by hackers. For example, it is not enough for a hospital to say that they took the normal standard of care in their industry—they will be called upon to show that they took every reasonable precaution. It also takes years to overcome the loss of safety credibility to employees and the local community.

Taking the right steps ahead of time, and equipping your facility and employees with the training, knowledge, and tools they need to prevent an attack and deal with one when it occurs may save lives. If you think I'm kidding, read about how a hacker can degrade or destroy your building equipment in the following chapters. If your building is connected to the Internet (directly or indirectly), a hacker may be able to install ransomware and take complete control of your building.

Take my advice and do the following:

- Completely disconnect your building controls system from the Internet immediately.

- Segregate the BCS from all other computer networks.

- Remove all modems and wireless cards from all computers, printers, and servers.

- Stop vendors from connecting remotely to your BCS. If they must connect to the BCS for maintenance, allow vendors to only use your laptops. These are laptops that stay in the building under lock and key and that are scanned for malware before and after they are used.

Have a professional perform a vulnerability assessment and report the results directly to top management. If you do these things, you will be able to sleep at night. Don't be "that guy."

---

[2]Shanker, Thom. "Test Errors Caused Chernobyl, Soviets Say" *Chicago Tribune*, August 22, 1986.

▨ **Hand-Off-Auto Switch (H-O-A)**   A device that has switches that maintain their position. Start and Stop buttons have momentary actions. The Off position prevents any operation. Used in a situation that has a single point of manual control to allow the motor (or other device) to (A) operate from an automated building control system, (O) not operate, or (H) operate with no safeguards or automated control. The Hand position is used to bump the motor or to operate for shorts times while observed by operating personnel.

I wrote this book because I searched unsuccessfully for cyber-physical attack recovery procedures specifically written for building controls or SCADA. I only found recovery plans when a hacker steals information or defaces websites. I did not find any that specifically address how to stop a cyber-physical attack intended to damage building equipment or how to react after a building has been attacked. This book should give you an idea how bad things can get, and how serious a problem a well-planned cyber-physical attack can be. Throughout this book, I use jargon taken from electrical and mechanical engineering fields as well as information technology and physical security environments. I include a definition of some terms that readers may not be familiar with in a text box or footnote. Otherwise, most definitions can be found in another book I wrote, the *Cybersecurity Lexicon* (Apress, 2016).

This book contains step-by-step instructions, checklists, and forms that you can use to develop your own Cyber-Physical Attack Recovery Procedures. Just as no two buildings are alike, no two Recovery Procedures are alike. Only a Recovery Procedures document that has been prepared by qualified engineers for your specific facility should be implemented. The appendix is merely a suggested template to be customized for your specific facility. A soft copy of the template is available for download (with fillable fields) on the Apress web page for this book (www.apress.com/9781484220641).

This book is not a crisis management plan. It is not a COOP plan (Continuity of Operations Plan). It is not a business continuity plan, IT application response plan, or an IT infrastructure response plan. Those are designed to prepare for a cyber-attack on an enterprise IT system (database) or organize a response team prior to a natural disaster. Other folks have already written those.

This book assumes hackers have already gained entry to your building controls. I describe the damage hackers can do, and suggest how maintenance personnel should respond to avoid prolonging the attack, and how to recover from the attack. The Recovery Procedures document is a *template* for *you* to modify based on the specific equipment in your facility with instructions on how to restore building equipment to normal operation when systems begin to act erratically, or fail completely. When hackers shut off the building water, turn off the power, disable the sewage effluent pumps, and activate the fire alarm, you have to do something quick. You won't have time to figure out the proper Sequence of Operations for your boilers and chillers. You need to quickly turn things off before a hacker can do any more damage. And, hackers can damage multiple systems in multiple buildings at the same time—from the other side of the planet. This book will help you create custom checklists for your equipment.

Normally, the response to a physical attack and the speed with which security staff reacts is a function of the type of attack. For example, a well-trained security force is able to respond to an active shooter in mere seconds. Unfortunately, a professional hacker can disable multiple pieces of critical building equipment in milliseconds, so monitoring the BCS for precursors of a cyber-physical attack, and an automated response based on intrusion detection is essential to prevent damage to expensive building equipment.

To make matters worse, unlike an active shooter who is no longer a threat once he has been dealt with, a hacker's handiwork persists long after you've cut the cord, and a hacker can continue to damage your equipment even if he no longer is in direct communication with the building controls system. A "sneaky" hacker (as Jack Nicholson says, "Is there another kind?") will install cyber booby-traps before making his presence known. Before maintenance personnel sound the all-clear, they will have to isolate each and every piece of equipment from the BCS and be prepared to operate all systems manually—just like the old days. Maintenance personnel will have to go to the equipment to read dials, turn valves and open dampers to bring the building back on line—safely.

Lastly, I want to mention the business case for putting Recovery Procedures in place for when a cyber-physical attack occurs. The cost to replace a 2 MW diesel backup generator is at least $2 million. An average chiller costs $200,000; a medium-size boiler probably $600,000. Normally, replacing any of these would take six months because these are long lead items. You may be able to repair some damaged equipment—provided you can get parts. Another thing to consider is that you will likely not be the only one attacked. Once the floodgates open and all-out cyber warfare begins, you will be ordering equipment at the same time as other victims of cyber-physical attacks.

■ **Blamestorming**   Figuring out who to blame when something goes wrong.

Oh, one more thing that I forgot to mention. An adversary can cause physical damage to your facilities, but there is another aspect to their activities that needs attention. The fact is, hackers are monitoring your company activities using your building controls and other building-related systems that your IT and security staff are probably unaware even exist.

CHAPTER 1

■ ■ ■

Cyber-Physical Attack Recovery Procedures

Many industrial facilities can have downtime costs of more than one million dollars per day. Equipment replacement times can easily be months. SCADA (Supervisory Control and Data Acquisition) systems, Building Control System (BCS), Industrial Control Systems (ICS), and Utility Control Systems (UCS) are extremely complex systems that require engineers and maintenance personnel to learn a new language. It's not enough anymore to simply know what a centrifugal chiller does and how a boiler works. Today, building maintenance personnel also need to know how hackers can attack critical equipment and damage critical infrastructure. Why? Because most building equipment today is computer-controlled and SCADA protocols are insecure by design. That means:

- Control systems protocols have little or no security safeguards

- Migration to TCP/IP networks with its inherent vulnerabilities

- Increased demand for remote diagnostics and maintenance access

- Interconnection with enterprise networks

- Legacy operating systems and applications with poor patching procedures

- Little monitoring of control systems for evidence of hacker presence

- Vendors not securing their product offerings adequately

- The majority of PLCs are ordered with web services enabled and most users leave unused web servers active (not configured), with factory default passwords

- Increased interest in control systems by foreign governments and terrorists

- Evidence that nation-states have already penetrated control systems

- Legacy industrial controls do not have the chip sets and processing capability to authenticate commands or identify malware

Historically, ordinary *cyber-attacks* were often undetectable and untraceable. A major *cyber-physical attack*, on the other hand is difficult to hide because building equipment is failing in real time. This is what happens if you want all the benefits of being "connected." This book focuses on the damage hackers that *can do* to building equipment and how they can really ruin your day. I describe potential ways to stop a cyber-physical attack, and then how to restore equipment operation without doing further damage.

Electronic supplementary material The online version of this chapter (doi:10.1007/978-1-4842-2065-8_1) contains supplementary material, which is available to authorized users.

Most companies cannot function without a physical presence—be it an office or a manufacturing facility. Large companies tend to link their facilities together in the "cloud," not realizing that an attack on one facility can quickly spread to many others. The Repository of Industrial Security Incidents (RISI) claims that the number of incidents directly affecting SCADA controls systems (accidental and malicious) has increased by 20 percent over the last ten years.

In 2005, the Zotob worm attacked 175 companies, including Caterpillar, General Electric, UPS, and Chrysler. At Chrysler, the Zotob worm shut down 13 assembly lines, idling 50,000 employees. Chrysler had professionally installed firewalls between the Internet and the company's network, but the worm was able to travel from plant to plant in seconds. Poor systems design and a failure to contain communications are other key problems. For example, upgrading the business system at the Hatch nuclear reactor zeroed out the control system database, causing the reactor safety system to interpret this as a drop in water cooling levels and triggering a shutdown that took two days to restore.

If your facilities controls systems are not segregated, it's only a matter of time before they *all* go down. Hackers only need to find vulnerabilities at one site to take them all down. It goes without saying that it is a crime to commit a cyber-physical attack, so preservation of evidence is important, but in my world (facilities), it is more important to restore normal building operations quickly.

Purpose of the Recovery Procedures

The purpose of the Cyber-Physical Attack Recovery Procedures (hereinafter referred to as the "Recovery Procedures") is to stop a cyber-physical attack and restore mission-critical processes (and the controls system) when an attack causes equipment to fail. I assume that you did *not* take my advice and your BCS is still connected to the Internet; it has modems, embedded web servers, and wireless routers; and vendors happily log in remotely to equipment (that I recommended you secure) or they regularly bring personal laptops to your mechanical rooms and plug into your BCS with little or no supervision. This book presents examples of cyber-physical attacks that hackers will attempt against your building equipment, so that your maintenance personnel understand the vulnerabilities and are prepared to respond to a cyber-physical incident.

■ **Embedded web server**   Web server software built into a building control system device that is provided to configure the device from a web browser. Also used remotely by equipment vendors to update software or troubleshoot problems.

This is an important point because when you ask a maintenance engineer if it is possible to *disable the safety controls* on a steam boiler so the fuel doesn't cut off automatically when the flame goes out or when the feedwater is stopped, the reply is usually: "Sure, but why would you want to?"

The Recovery Procedures Template in the Appendix contains generic forms to be customized for your specific building controls. They serve as the central repository for the information, tasks, and procedures that would be necessary to restore critical equipment functions. Having this information readily at hand is especially important because a cyber-physical attack on a building control system is engineered such that a prompt resumption of operations cannot be accomplished by employing normal daily operating procedures. This is not business as usual.

When a cyber-physical attack strikes, you won't be able to simply log on to a vendor website and download the latest drivers. Vendor websites will experience denial of service attacks to prevent you and others like you from recovering after the attacks. If you don't have hard copy of the network diagrams, equipment operation manuals, rescue CD-ROMs and original vendor software, you will be out of luck.

Why do I need Cyber-Physical Attack Recovery Procedures? Can't we just disconnect the Internet and turn the equipment back on?

First of all, when a cyber-physical attack is verified, I recommend you *physically pull the computer's power plug from the wall* rather than gracefully shutting down. Forensic data can be destroyed if the operating system executes a normal shutdown process. Also, avoid running any antivirus software "after the fact" as the antivirus scan changes critical file dates and impedes discovery and analysis of suspected malicious files and timelines. Secondly, a well-designed and coordinated cyber-physical attack will include *cyber booby-traps* intended to continue to cause damage when maintenance personnel attempt to restore normal equipment operation.

■ **Cyber booby-trap**   When a hacker embeds malware that is triggered by actions of the building maintenance staff. For example, the initial indication of a cyber-attack may be that the hacker turned off the water to a boiler. The maintenance personnel in the control room are unaware that the malware pumped all the water out of the boiler and turned up the heat. Once the boiler is superheated, the action of turning on the water triggers an explosion. The hacker needed the triggering action by building maintenance personnel to maximize the damage.

Cyber booby-traps are "scripts" (similar to a macro) planted by a hacker that are unknowingly triggered by the actions of the building maintenance personnel such as switching something on or off triggering hidden malware. A hacker is counting on maintenance personnel to behave in a way that allows the cyber-physical attack to continue well after the back door access has been lost. If you put *your* Recovery Procedures on a server that can be hacked, the exact sequence of operations maintenance personnel plan to follow will be known by hackers well in advance. The hacker will then use your procedures against you. In essence, your maintenance personnel would be doing his work for him after you think you are safe.

With this foreknowledge in hand, a hacker "engineers" a *specific* cyber-physical attack scenario for your facility, and he is depending on the triggers that he "scripted" to continue the attack. *Without those triggers, the cyber-physical attack can be halted.* Don't waste time trying to find the hidden triggers. Unplug the BCS server and return to a fully manual operation, and you disrupt scripted cyber booby-traps.

It's important to understand that the goal of a hacker is to cause severe damage to critical systems and the malware used is very sophisticated. Simply powering equipment back up after disconnecting the BCS from the Internet does not mean you are out of the woods. *You've been hacked* and the Barbarians are no longer outside the gates. They are already inside your controls system and they depend on you to follow their script to prolong the attack after the back doors they planted have been shut.

Cyber booby-trap designs vary depending on the trigger mechanism, the payload and the amount of damage a hacker intends to cause (and when). A cyber booby-trap can react with zero delay or it can be programmed with time delays to confuse maintenance personnel. Unlike standard ordnance, such as an artillery shell, grenade, or high explosive, cyber booby-traps use your building equipment as the "payload" to do the damage. Part of the skill in placing cyber booby-traps lies in exploiting natural human behaviors such as habit, curiosity, or inquisitiveness, or by providing maintenance personnel what appears to be a simple solution to a vexing problem.

Almost any piece of building equipment can be cyber booby-trapped in some way. The only limits to the intricacy of cyber booby-traps are the skill and inventiveness of the hackers placing them. For example, fake pressure reading displays on a natural gas line can be used as "bait." The "bait object" that lures victims into a cyber booby-trap in the sequence of operations to restart a boiler may not even be designed to affect boiler operations at all. Instead, the boiler restart attempt may activate other hidden cyber booby-traps designed to damage chillers, air-handling units, building lighting, or set off false fire alarms.

Cyber booby-traps are planted in any situation where there is a strong likelihood of them being encountered and triggered by maintenance personnel—especially on critical systems or equipment maintenance personnel are forced to use. In order to ensure damage to critical pieces of equipment, a hacker will install many cyber booby-traps, each one initiates a particular set of "undesirable events". You will have multiple attacks simultaneously.

When a cyber booby-trap is triggered, it can cause equipment to go into "defect" mode. It can turn equipment on or off, change configuration set points, change motor speeds, increase or decrease fluid pressure, or any number of things. A cyber booby-trap can cause computer displays to go blank or indicate false information about equipment performance. Equipment can be made to operate erratically; software can be modified so when maintenance personnel enter a command to decrease water pressure, the BCS actually increases the water pressure. Or, an attempt to silence one alarm causes other alarms to annunciate. Knowing that hackers are capable of planting cyber booby-traps in a BCS is only the first step in determining how to respond to a cyber-attack.

■ **Canary**   Anything that can send up an observable alert if something happens. For example, you can set up a computer on a subnet such that no other computer should ever access that. If something touches it, you know it's from outside normal behavior. Also called a *tripwire*.

On the flip side, you can *set some "traps" of your own* to alert you when hackers are lurking in the shadows such as a canary or a honeypot. You can program setpoint traps, such as a specific temperature range for a certain area, to restrict override changes from going outside of set parameters and include PIN control on user access to system changes. You can also use a timed feature to automatically revert to original settings after a temporary override period.

In terms of personnel and financial resources, the information, tasks and procedures detailed in this Recovery Procedure represents a commitment to response, resumption, recovery, and restoration planning. Therefore, it is essential that the information and actions in this Recovery Procedure remain viable and it be maintained in a state of currency in order to ensure the accuracy of its contents. The Recovery Procedures must be stored securely. It is incumbent upon every individual who is in receipt of the Recovery Procedures, or who has a role in implementing them ensure that sufficient attention is given to the security of the document. Since the information contained in the Recovery Procedures describes planning assumptions and objectives, it should be considered a sensitive document.

■ **Honeypot**   A system (e.g., a web server) or a system resource (e.g., a file on a server) that is designed to be attractive to potential crackers and intruders and has no authorized users other than its administrators. (Source: CNSSI-4009)

The Recovery Procedures are intended to provide a framework for constructing plans to ensure the safety of employees and the resumption of time-sensitive operations and services. Although the Recovery Procedures provides guidance and documentation upon which to base emergency response, resumption, and recovery planning efforts, it is not intended as a substitute for informed decision-making. Customized Recovery Procedures should include detailed responsibilities and specific tasks for emergency response activities and building resumption operations based upon pre-defined time frames.

Preparing Recovery Procedures and presenting them to management may satisfy the immediate need of having a documented plan. However, this is not enough if the goal is to have a viable response, resumption, recovery, and restoration capability. In order to establish that capability, plans and the activities associated with their maintenance (i.e., training, revision, and exercising) must become an integral part of building maintenance operations.

A Recovery Procedures document is not a one-time commitment with a fixed start and end date. It should be an ongoing, properly funded security activity intended to provide required resources to:

- Perform activities required to construct recovery and restoration plans

- Train and retrain employees

- Develop and revise policies and standards as the cyber threat environment evolves

- Exercise strategies, procedures, team, and resources requirements

- Re-exercise unattained exercise objectives

- Report ongoing continuity planning to senior management

- Research processes and technologies to improve resumption and recovery efficiency

- Perform plan maintenance activities

Developing Recovery Procedures that encompass activities required to maintain a viable continuity capability require a consistent planning methodology. Recovery Procedure elements necessary to create a viable, repeatable and verifiable continuity capability include:

- Implementing accurate and continuous vital records, data backup, and off-site storage

- Implementing capabilities for rapid disconnect of communication circuits

- Providing alternate manual controls for equipment operations

- Constructing a contingency organization

- Implementing contingency strategies

Cyber-Physical Attack Timetable

This is the timetable hackers follow in preparation for a cyber-attack. They begin with reconnaissance of the target. The adversary decides to target your facilities and investigates the attack surface looking for vulnerabilities. Open source web mining against your corporate websites, those of vendors that support your facilities, as well as online conference attendee lists gives the attacker as much information about your facilities as your maintenance personnel have. The adversary maps your building controls network and formulates an attack strategy using open source information about your organization, your facilities and your personnel. If you are a Fortune 500 company in the United States, *this step is already complete*, especially if your business is a direct competitor or if you support the Department of Defense.

Once the adversary has an attack strategy, he will begin to weaponize a set of attack tools and develop a package for delivery and execution on your building controls network. The adversary creates a repository of cyber-physical attack tools that use several zero-day vulnerabilities specifically designed to cause significant damage to your facilities and ensure that your buildings take months to repair. Again, if you are a Fortune 500 company in the United States, *this step is already complete* and the adversary established a regimen to check his back doors periodically to ensure his ability to deliver the payload on demand.

When the adversary gets the green light to deliver the packaged attack tool or tools to the target, he is ready to commence the attack. He may already have installed the attack tools (malware) in your system without your knowledge. Although not easily hidden, it can be overlooked by understaffed personnel not looking for hidden malware that has not been activated yet.

When the adversary gets a green light to commence an initial attack the malware is executed. The attack can be a test to see if your staff is able to detect their presence or it could be designed to solicit a ransom. If it is a full-scale attack intended to destroy costly equipment at multiple locations, it's probably a nation-state and not script kiddies. Welcome to the Big Leagues.

When a full-scale cyber-physical attack occurs, a sneaky adversary will have designed the cyber-physical attack in a manner that relies on the victim's maintenance personnel following the response or recovery plan that he already stole. The attack is scripted so your maintenance personnel will cause more damage to the equipment, spread the attack to other facilities, and possibly create more back doors. Your facilities will be down for months and cost millions to repair.

Recovery Procedures Information

The Recovery Procedures contain static information (information that remains constant and not subject to frequent revisions) and dynamic information (information that must be updated regularly). The static information should be read and understood by all employees, users, and building administrators, and by all individuals involved in any phase of emergency response, resumption, recovery, or restoration. The dynamic information requires frequent review and modification to keep up with the changing cyber-threat environment.

The dynamic information should reside in a Computer-Aided Facility Management (CAFM) database and printed as output for your Recovery Procedures. By using the CAFM database, dynamic information that is vital to the survival of the building control system will be easy to manage and update. The CAFM database often includes unencrypted contact lists, emergency procedures, and technical components and as such, the CAFM database *must not* be accessible from the Internet. Why make it easy for hackers to know what you intend to do and how you plan to respond to a cyber-physical attack?

Although it is necessary to be familiar with the static information during recovery, it should not be necessary to read that information at the time of the event. The completed Recovery Procedures should provide all of the necessary lists, tasks, and reports used for response, resumption, or recovery.

Applicable Directives

In the federal government, the development of Recovery Procedures is required by executive directives and must meet regulatory mandates. Management must maintain an information assurance infrastructure that ensures that its information resources maintain availability, confidentiality, integrity, and non-repudiation of its data. Furthermore, management must protect their strategic information resources management capabilities. Therefore, this Cyber-Physical Attack Recovery Procedure was developed in accordance with the following executive decisions, regulatory mandates, provisions, and directives:

- Office of Management and Budget Circular A–130, Revised (Transmittal Memorandum No. 4), Appendix III, Security of Federal Automated Information Resources, November 2000.

- Computer Security Act of 1987, Public Law 100-235, January 1988.

- Presidential Decision Directive 63, Critical Infrastructure Protection, May 1998.

- Presidential Decision Directive 67, Enduring Constitutional Government and Continuity of Government Operations, October 1998.

- Executive Order 12656, Assignment of Emergency Preparedness Responsibilities, November 1988.

- Federal Information Processing Standards (FIPS) Publication 87, Guidelines for ADP Cyber-Attack Recovery Planning, March 1981.

- DOJ Order 2640.2D, Information Technology Security, July 12, 2001.

Objectives for a Plan

Organizations are dependent on a variety of IT systems classified as a general support system (GSS), which provide mission-critical functions of connectivity, Internet access, and email, or Major Applications (MAs) which are specific software programs written to produce output to fulfill the agency's service to its customers. Although many threats and vulnerabilities can be mitigated, some of the threats cannot be prevented. Therefore, it is important that the organization develop Recovery Procedures to ensure the uninterrupted existence of its business functions and in the case of government, continued service to the agency and the public.

The primary focus of a Recovery Procedure revolves around the protection of two important assets of any organization: personnel and equipment. All facets of Recovery Procedures should address the protection and safety of personnel and the protection and recovery of equipment to full operation. This includes establishing an operational capability to process pre-designated critical applications, recovering data from off-site backup data sets, and restoring the affected building systems to normal operational status. The Recovery Procedures seeks to accomplish the following additional objectives:

- Minimize the number of decisions that must be made during a cyber-physical attack

- Identify the resources needed to execute the actions defined by this plan

- Identify actions to be undertaken by pre-designated recovery teams

- Identify critical data in conjunction with customers that will be recovered during the Hot Site phase of recovery operations

- Define the process for testing and maintaining the procedures and training for contingencies

Incident Response Teams

In the event of a cyber-physical attack, the normal operation of the organization will shift into that of a contingency organization. The focus of the building control system will shift from the current structure and function of "business as usual" to the structure and function of a building control system working toward the resumption of time-sensitive building operations. In this Recovery Procedure, the organization's building maintenance personnel, IT staff and security personnel will operate in Incident Response Teams (IRT) through the phases of detection, mitigation, and recovery. Each phase requires the teams executing those procedures to work together closely. Each of the teams is comprised of individuals with specific responsibilities, which must be completed to fully execute the plan. There will be at least four teams: the Recovery Management Team, the Facilities Team, the Security Team, and the Tech Support Team. Primary and alternate team leaders are named during the preparation of the Recovery Procedures documents to lead each team.

Each team becomes a sub-unit of the organization's contingency organization and the teams are structured to provide dedicated, focused support in the areas of their particular experience and expertise for specific response, resumption and recovery tasks, responsibilities, and objectives. Each team's eventual goal is the resumption/recovery and the return to stable and normal building operations. Status and progress updates will be reported by each team leader to a Recovery Procedures Coordinator.

The Incident Recovery Team's primary duties are as follows:

- To protect employees and equipment until normal building operations are resumed.

- To ensure that a viable capability exists to respond to a cyber-physical attack.

- To manage all response, resumption, recovery, and restoration activities.

- To support and communicate with employees, system administrators, security officers, and managers.

- To accomplish rapid and efficient resumption of time-sensitive building operations, technology, and functional support areas.

- To ensure regulatory requirements are satisfied.

- To exercise resumption and recovery expenditure decisions.

- To streamline the reporting of resumption and recovery progress between the teams and management of each system.

Recovery Management Team (MGMT)

The Incident Recovery Management Team is headed by the Recovery Procedures Coordinator and is responsible for the administrative, supply and public relations portions of the recovery process. The sub-team leaders report to this team during a cyber-physical attack. Each of these responsibilities should be headed by a member of the MGMT.

General Activities

The Incident Recovery Management Team is responsible for the following:

- Assess the damage and if necessary, declare a cyber-physical attack (damage assessment forms are included in this plan)
- Coordinate efforts of all teams
- Approve all actions that were not preplanned
- Give strategic direction
- Be the liaison to upper management
- Expedite matters through all bureaucracy
- Provide counseling to those employees that request or require it.

Procedures by Phase

The Incident Recovery Management Team performs the following duties in these phases:

Phase 1: Detection

- Activate Incident Response Teams
- Initiate Rapid Inspections of building and systems
- Declare a Cyber-Physical Attack and notify upper management
- Decide whether building is safe to occupy or if it should be evacuated

Phase 2: Mitigation

- Establish the command center
- Evacuate the building if necessary
- Prioritize recovery efforts
- Coordinate activities of Incident Response Teams

Phase 3: Recovery

- Coordinate activities of Incident Response Teams
- Reoccupy the building and resume normal operations
- Inform management

Recovery Facilities Team (FAC)

The Facilities Team is responsible for minimizing the damage at the primary site once the Tech Support Team has pulled the plug on the BCS. The Facilities Team also makes a quick determination of what equipment is salvageable and what is not. Repair and replacement orders will be filed for what is not in working condition. The Facilities Team is responsible for locating the new building equipment needed and overseeing the replacement and construction.

Procedures by Phase

The Facilities Team performs the following duties in these phases:

Phase 1: Detection

- Mobilize Facilities Team
- Initiate Rapid Engineering Inspections of building and BCS devices

Phase 2: Mitigation

- Perform damage assessment
- Assist in the immediate salvage operations
- Determine the requirements for building equipment replacement
- Help determine what new computer and network hardware is needed
- Inventory all equipment in the building. If necessary, involve the equipment vendors

Phase 3: Recovery

- Salvage equipment and supplies
- Order new building equipment and computer hardware
- Arrange for installation and testing of the new hardware
- Work with contractors and agency staff to restore operations
- Oversee the installation of the new building equipment
- Ensure building equipment and controls are working as designed

Recovery Tech Support Team (TECH)

The Tech Support Team is responsible for the operation and maintenance of the BCS. The responsibility of the TECH Team is to acquire (along with the Facilities Team), configure, and install servers and workstations for the BCS. The TECH Team shall reconstruct and reconfigure the BCS software at the primary site. In addition, the TECH Team will provide technical support to the other teams.

Procedures by Phase

The Tech Support Team performs the following duties in these phases:

Phase 1: Detection

- Mobilize Tech Support Team
- Initiate Rapid Inspections of building control system

Phase 2: Mitigation

- Test the hardware and software
- Determine scope of damage for BCS servers and workstations
- Work with appropriate vendors

Phase 3: Recovery

- Order appropriate equipment and supplies (coordinate and work with the Facilities Team for this activity)
- Build servers and workstations
- Install and configure systems at the primary site
- Test the hardware and software
- Work with appropriate vendors to assist in recovery
- Verify that the systems are performing as expected

Recovery Security Team (SEC)

The Security Team (SEC) responsibilities include the physical security operations of the building and collecting, transporting and securing all IT servers and recent backup tapes for forensic examination. When a cyber-physical attack is declared, the security team must establish a chain-of-custody and secure the IT equipment and backup tapes for transport to the forensics facility. This team is also responsible for securing the building for the duration of the incident.

Procedures by Phase

The Security Team performs the following duties in these phases:

Phase 1: Detection

- Mobilize Security Team
- Initiate Rapid Inspections of building and secure building control system

Phase 2: Mitigation

- Inventory and secure the correct backup tapes
- Transport the servers and tapes to the forensics facility

Phase 3: Recovery

- Provide physical for security at the building
- Assist all teams in restoring the production environment
- Provide security escorts to construction personnel
- Provide temporary badging service for vendors and contractors
- Assist in reestablishing security and CCTV system to normal operation
- Monitor the building for unusual anomalous behavior
- Monitor deliveries
- Provide security escorts to movers

Recovery Phases

The Recovery Procedures Coordinator, in conjunction with building management determines which teams/ team members are responsible for each function during each phase. As tasking is assigned, additional responsibilities, teams, and task lists need to be created to address specific functions during a specific phase.

■ **Incident detection**   Ways in which a cyber-incident is identified and reported. Detecting most incidents requires automated analysis tools, system behavior patterns, and an awareness of what to look for among operators, supervisors, and other staff. The building equipment operators and the process engineers are usually critical to detection of unusual operations and are the first to note a difference in system behavior. Also called *discovery*.

Phase 1: Detection

- When anomalous behavior is observed such as multiple equipment failures, Intrusion Detection System alerts are sounded, or a catastrophic event occurs, the Incident Response Team consults the Event Diagnostics Table to determine if the "event" is a possible cyber-physical attack.
- The Incident Response Team then consults the Integrity Checks Table to verify if a cyber-physical attack is underway.
- To provide management with the facts necessary to make informed decisions regarding subsequent resumption and recovery activity.

■ **Intrusion Detection Systems (IDS)**   There are two types of IDS:

Host-based IDS operates on information collected from within an individual computer system. This vantage point allows host-based IDSs to determine exactly which processes and user accounts are involved in a particular attack on the Operating System. Furthermore, unlike network-based IDSs, host-based IDSs can more readily "see" the intended outcome of an attempted attack, because they can directly access and monitor the data files and system processes usually targeted by attacks. (Source: SP 800-36; CNSSI-4009)

Network-based IDS detects attacks by capturing and analyzing network packets. Listening on a network segment or switch, one network-based IDS can monitor the network traffic affecting multiple hosts that are connected to the network segment. (Source: SP 800-36; CNSSI-4009)

Phase 2: Mitigation

- The Incident Response Team's first priority is to isolate any compromised devices and protect the building and personnel through segmentation. The segmentation must be based on a predetermined strategy taking into account specific equipment and building mission realities. After this step is complete, the Incident Response Team ensures that local control has been achieved.

- The facilities Incident Response Team conducts a preliminary assessment of incident impact, known injuries, extent of damage, and disruption to the building services and operations.

- The Incident Response Team informs the Recovery Procedures Coordinator who determines if or when access to the facility will be allowed.

- The Recovery Procedures Coordinator establishes and organizes a management control center and headquarters for the recovery operations.

- The Recovery Procedures Coordinator implements procedures necessary to mobilize operations, support and department relocation as well as employee and external individuals and organizations notification before, during, and after relocation.

- The Recovery Procedures Coordinator notifies and appraises management of the situation.

■ **Safety instrumented system**   A building control system that uses control devices and sensors designed to put the system in a safe state when predetermined conditions are violated. Also called an *emergency shutdown system* (ESS), a *safety shutdown system* (SSD), and a *safety interlock system* (SIS).

Phase 3: Recovery

- The Incident Response Teams execute investigations, incident response plans, and various other overarching command guidelines prior to executing any recovery actions. They implement procedures necessary to facilitate and support the recovery of time-sensitive building operations.

- The Recovery Phase begins once the system under attack has been stabilized and infected equipment has been isolated from the BCS network. Replacement of infected devices with off-the-shelf replacements ensures that recovered devices are uncontaminated when reintegrated into the network and will aid in preservation of forensic evidence of the cyber-attack.

- The Incident Response Teams coordinate with employees, vendors, and other internal and external individuals and organizations.

Assumptions

All assumptions that the Recovery Procedures will hinge on must be documented. This could range from absolutely necessary conditions to helpful information in support of the Recovery Procedures phases such as that all necessary Memorandums of Agreement (MOAs) and Memorandums of Understanding (MOUs) have been executed.

Critical Success Factors

This section addresses the factors and issues that specifically apply to the Recovery Procedures that have been identified to be critical to the successful implementation of the Recovery Procedures. These factors are as follows:

- Commitment by senior management to Cyber-Physical Attack Planning and Recovery.

- Budgetary commitment to Cyber-Physical Attack Planning and Recovery.

- Modifications and improvements to the current scheduling procedures for the retention and transportation of back up files to the offsite storage facility.

- Development and execution of the necessary memorandums of agreement (MOAs), memorandums of understanding (MOUs), and service level agreements (SLAs).

- Procurement of an alternate power source.

Mission Critical Systems

Table 1-1 lists essential mission critical systems/applications/services that must be recovered at the time of disaster in the following order due to critical interdependencies.

Table 1-1. *Essential Systems*

Systems Acronym	System Name
BCS	Building Control System
UMCS	Utility Management Controls System
EMCS	Energy Management Controls System
CMMS	Computerized Maintenance Management System
CAFM	Computer-Aided Facility Management

Figure 1-1 indicates the recovery process.

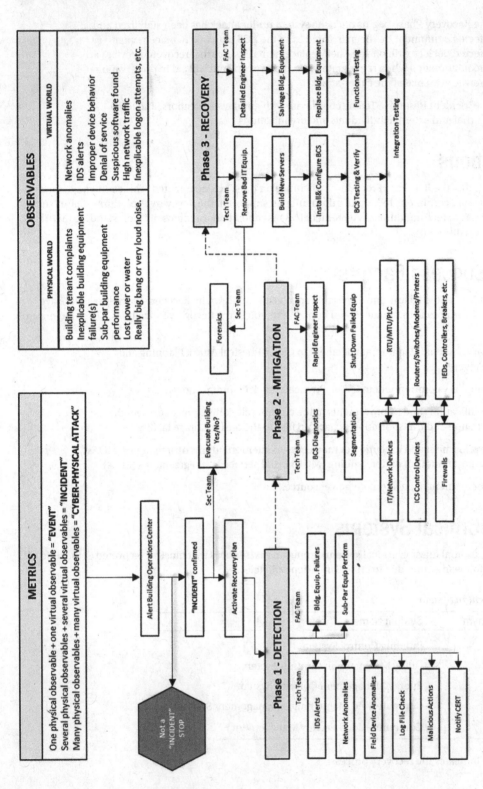

***Figure 1-1.** The recovery process Mission critical systems*

14

CHAPTER 2

■ ■ ■

Threats and Attack Detection

When developing strategies for Recovery Procedures, it is helpful to consider the entire range of possible and probable cyber-physical attack vectors that present a risk to an organization. From that range of threats, likely scenarios can be developed and appropriate strategies applied. Any Recovery Procedures should be designed to be flexible enough to respond to extended building interruptions, as well as major natural disasters.

The best way to achieve this goal is to design Recovery Procedures that could be used to address a major natural disaster, but is divided into sections that can be used to address extended building interruptions. While each of the identified attack vectors could result in a disaster by itself, in a major cyber-physical attack, several attack vectors will be used concurrently or occur sequentially, depending on the circumstances.

As a result, it is advisable to develop several levels of strategies that can be applied as needed. For example, a power outage in the computing center may render that equipment unusable. An appropriate strategy for that event may be temporary relocation of personnel to another building. An event that requires temporary evacuation of the computer center, such as a loss of chilled water to the cooling system that may take several days to resolve, may necessitate switchover capabilities and possible regional mirrored redundancy capabilities that would be transparent to the users.

An event of greater magnitude, such as an explosion, may render the entire building unusable for an extended period of time and might necessitate a strategy based on mirrored redundancy as well as a secondary strategy involving a secondary hot site. Time sensitivity and mission criticality in conjunction with budgetary limitations, level of threat and degree of risk will be major factors in the development of recommended strategies.

Probable Threats

You will hear security professionals say it's impossible to prevent a committed adversary from penetrating your defense, but you need to consider who the adversary could be. There are several classes of adversaries in the cyber-physical realm with varying degrees of expertise.

- *Script kiddies*: Amateurs capable of downloading "canned" attack tools. Relatively unsophisticated, but dangerous nonetheless. Easily defeated by an effective patch management protocol and basic cyber-hygiene.

- *Criminals*: Seasoned IT professionals capable of hacking into enterprise networks and carrying out denial of service attacks, stealing bank account information or locking a hard drive for ransom.

- *Foreign security service (FSS)*: Advanced persistent threat, not interested in denial of service attacks or bitcoin ransom pocket change. Their goal is intelligence, surveillance, and reconnaissance (ISR)—however, a future goal may be to take down an entire nation's power grid or energy infrastructure.

© Luis Ayala 2016
L. Ayala, *Cyber-Physical Attack Recovery Procedures*, DOI 10.1007/978-1-4842-2065-8_2

Air-gap computers, firewalls, DMZ, network nodes, multi-factor authentication, and encrypted communications should prevent script kiddies from taking out your building equipment. Those defenses will probably also discourage criminals from trying to get in because it's easier to try the doorknob next door than invest time and energy in trying to defeat a well-defended network.

The only one you need to worry about is the foreign security service. These defenses may not be 100 percent effective against well-trained and well-funded nation states, but the number of nations capable of defeating all these defenses can probably be counted on one hand. These defenses will stop or slow down second-tier nation-states from getting into your network long enough for you to react to an attack.

■ **Cyber-attack tree** A conceptual diagram showing how a computer system might be attacked by describing the threats and possible cyber-attacks to realize those threats. Cyber-attack trees lend themselves to defining an information assurance strategy and are increasingly being applied to industrial control systems and the electric power grid. Executing a strategy changes the cyber-attack tree.

Depending on the type of facility being attacked, the biggest targets of a cyber-attack are the building utilities (electricity, water, gas, sewer), and heating, ventilation, and air conditioning (HVAC) systems. Other targets listed in Table 2-1 are secondary in that they are less likely to result in catastrophic failure and a life safety consideration.

Table 2-1. Probability of Attacks[1]

Probability of Threats: Cyber-Attack Trees			
	High	Medium	Low
Boiler Explosion			X
Power Interruption	XX		
Air Conditioning Failure	XX		
Loss of Water		X	
Communications Loss	X		
Fire		X	
Loss of Office Lighting	X		
Interrupt Security Cameras		X	
Set Off Alarm Systems	X		
Unlock Doors			X
Heating System Failure	X		
Data Destruction	X		
Gas Pressure Vessel Failure			X
Carbon Monoxide Poisoning		X	
Natural Gas Fuel Train Damage			X

---

[1]While a terrorist may want to cause a boiler to explode, he would have to know a great deal about the particular installation to be able to pull it off. It's low probability because a script kiddie can't do it.

A cyber-physical attack against a well-defended target is extremely difficult to do so there is a very strong likelihood that if your building is attacked, the attack originated in a foreign country, probably by a foreign security service. Generally speaking, criminal groups are not interested in shutting down building systems or utility grids because there is no profit in that. A cyber-physical attack designed to damage expensive, mission-critical equipment is probably intended to disrupt the economy of a country, not to steal information. That said, a foreign security service would likely employ cyber-physical attack engineering to create as much damage as possible. The hacker will look to cause the most damage as quickly as possible because he assumes you will quickly be on to him and disconnect the connection to disrupt the attack.

■ **Cyber-physical attack engineering**   Designing an attack scenario to exploit a particular physical process requires a solid engineering background and in-depth *destructive* knowledge of the target SCADA system. Hacking a chemical plant, for example, requires knowledge of physics, chemistry, and engineering, as well as a great deal about how the network is laid out, and a keen understanding of process-aware defensive systems. This represents a high (but not insurmountable) barrier to entry for garden-variety script kiddies, but is not a major obstacle for a foreign security service.

A hacker will attack a single point of failure first. He will attack a device or system that will cause other systems to fail. For example, shut off the water to the building and the mission will continue, albeit somewhat degraded. However, shut off the electricity and everything shuts down—eventually. If the hacker can damage the building switchgear or transformers, it won't matter if the uninterruptable power supply (UPS) works. It also won't matter if the backup generator fires up. Electricity will not be distributed properly through the building. What's worse is that large transformers today are manufactured overseas, so replacement of damaged equipment will take months. Your electrical engineers may say it can't be done, but we are dealing with very smart engineers funded by a foreign government and they've studied your building systems thoroughly and mapped your controls years ago.

■ **Flaw hypothesis methodology**   System analysis and penetration technique in which the specification and documentation for a building control system are analyzed to produce a list of hypothetical flaws. This list is prioritized on the basis of the estimated probability that a flaw exists, on the ease of exploiting it, and on the extent of control or compromise it would provide. The prioritized list is used to perform penetration testing of a building control system. (Source: CNSSI-4009)

Cyber-Physical Attack Detection

Although not always the case, past cyber-attacks have been analyzed and certain "precursors" have been detected, but many are easily ignored by building maintenance personnel. Let me be clear, unless absolutely necessary, your BCS should not be accessed from outside the building. However, if you *must* have remote access and connectivity, then whenever there are precursors indicating that a cyber-physical attack is imminent (such as increased port scanning or a rash of spear phishing attempts), *all* outside connections should be severed *immediately* as a precaution.

■ **Day zero** or **zero day**   is the day that a new cyber vulnerability is made known. In some cases, a zero-day exploit refers to an exploit for which no patch is available yet. ("day one" > day on which the patch is made available).

The first indication that a cyber-physical attack is underway might be BCS alarms sounding that a piece of building equipment has failed. A sophisticated attack will use several zero-day vulnerabilities so antivirus solutions looking for known malware signatures won't detect it. Automated detection via applications or routines, such as network monitors, network traffic analysis applications, IDS, and antivirus programs that can detect and flag malware, intrusion attempts, policy violations, and exploits may help determine the actual presence of hackers, but equipment failure and user observation of abnormal system or component behavior will likely appear first.

■ **Gray hole attack**   A type of **packet drop attack** in which a router that is supposed to relay packets instead discards them for a particular network destination, at a certain time of the day, a packet every n packets or every t seconds, or a randomly selected portion of the packets. This usually occurs from a router becoming compromised from a number of different causes. Because packets are routinely dropped from a lossy network, a packet drop attack is very hard to detect and prevent.

Building maintenance personnel, equipment operators, or process engineers will likely know before IT system administrators that a cyber-physical attack is underway. Experienced building maintenance personnel are the best source of detecting abnormal behavior, because subtle differences in equipment operation may create a "just doesn't feel right" atmosphere. Experienced equipment operators will know when things are not working right and can detect potential cyber-intrusions as well as or better than automated intrusion detection systems.

■ **Indicator**   A recognized action (specific, generalized, or theoretical) that an adversary might be expected to take in preparation for an attack. (Source: CNSSI-4009)

Table 2-2 contains a list of symptoms that could be considered *indicators of a cyber-physical attack* was taken from NIST SP 800-82, "Guide to Industrial Control Systems (ICS) Security (Final Public Draft)," September 2008.

Table 2-2. *Indicators of a Possible Cyber-Physical Attack*

- Unusually heavy network traffic
- Out of disk space or significantly reduced free disk space
- Unusually high CPU usage
- Creation of new user accounts
- Attempted or actual use of administrator-level accounts
- Locked-out accounts
- Accounts in use when the user is not at work
- Cleared log files
- Full log files with an unusually large number of events
- Antivirus or IDS alerts

(*continued*)

Table 2-2. (*continued*)

- Disabled antivirus software and other security controls
- Unexpected patch changes
- Machines or intelligent field devices connecting to outside IP addresses
- Requests for information about the system (social engineering attempts)
- Unexpected changes in configuration settings
- Unexpected system shutdown
- Other possible indicators of a cyber incident include:
- Stoppage or displayed error messages on a web, database, or application server
- Unusually slow access to hosts on the network
- Filenames containing unusual characters or new or unexpected files and directories
- Auditing configuration changes logged on the host records, especially disabling of auditing functionality
- A large number of bounced e-mails with suspicious content
- Unusual deviation from typical network traffic flows
- Erratic equipment behavior, especially when more than one device exhibits the same behavior
- Any apparent override of safety, backup, or failover systems
- Equipment, servers, or network traffic that has bursts of temporary high usage when the operational process itself is steady and predictable.
- Unknown or unusual traffic from corporate or other network external to control systems network
- Unknown or unexpected firmware pulls or pushes

Intrusion Detection Systems (IDS) designed to *detect an out-of-range or targeted event* can be defeated by a hacker merely by changing the configuration profile in the BCS. An IDS compares character strings with matches to known virus signatures or certain network behavior, such as a denial-of-service attack. An IDS may detect attempts to access certain restricted ports, or it may recognize a known rogue IP source address. With individual BCS components, it could be a customized application that detects anomalous software behavior or when the equipment goes outside preset setpoints and thresholds. Keep in mind that even a very good IDS is no guarantee of invulnerability, as seen with a Cinderella Attack.

■ **Cinderella attack**   A cyber-attack that disables security software by manipulating the network internal clock time so that a security software license expires, prematurely rendering the target network vulnerable to cyber-attack.

ABNORMAL SITUATION MANAGEMENT

Abnormal situation management (ASM) was developed with the goal of improving safety and performance in process plants. Over the past 20 years, the ASM Consortium has developed knowledge, tools, and products designed to prevent and manage abnormal situations in the process industry. This knowledge is directly applicable to cyber-physical attack response. For example, annunciation of more alarms in a given period of time than a human operator can respond is known as **alarm flooding**. Ten alarms per minute are typically the most alarms that a technician can handle. Assuming the BCS is set up using **alarm filtering**, the technician concentrates on the equipment failure that caused the cascade of subsequent failures.

■ **Alarm filtering**   A times, failure of one piece of building equipment may cause another piece of equipment to fail. Alarm filtering reports the original failure with more priority than subsequent failures showing the technician which equipment to repair first.

A well-planned cyber-physical attack is a dynamic process and the speed of the response will determine the extent of recovery requirements. ASM studies have shown that the total alarm resolution lag for a trained technician is typically 10 minutes (see the following diagram).

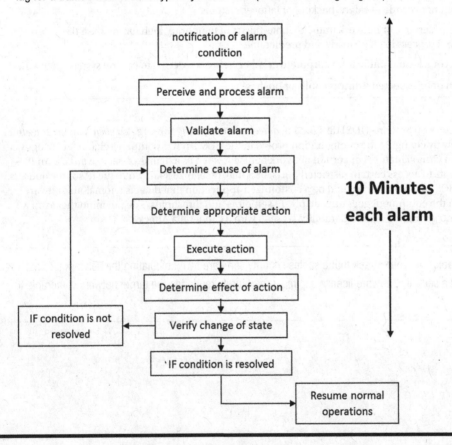

Detecting an event is only the beginning; the IDS must present the data in a useful format. Advanced IDS includes automated filtering and reporting features; others may just write log information to a text file. The ideal situation would be to set ranges and report only when conditions exist that are outside the range.

Some sophisticated systems like an *intrusion prevention system* (IPS) are designed to take some preventative actions without human intervention. However, most IPS are designed for well-understood IT applications and not for a production BCS where inadvertent shutdowns could have undesirable results. A human must be involved to decipher false-positives and to separate maintenance issues from potential cyber-physical attacks. The human also must be able to respond to the data and initiate the appropriate response quickly.

Incident Response Tools

Various automated tools are available to detect a potential cyber-physical attack during routine operations. The following are some examples:

- *Netflow capture and analysis.* These tools provide methods to capture and display the type of traffic crossing the network, including inbound and outbound traffic. They can isolate data by applications, conversations, domains, endpoints, and protocols. Many also store data for both analysis and forensics.

- *Network performance monitors.* These tools provide insight into network performance and can help identify where out-of-normal performance is occurring.

- *Availability monitors.* These tools can assist in determining if network devices are available with advanced "ping" capabilities or "heartbeat signals."

- *Application monitors.* A specific application can be monitored if there is suspicion of unauthorized access or manipulation. These tools allow a more granular analysis of a suspected application as compared with overall network monitoring.

- *Packet and traffic reconstructors.* These tools reconstruct files back into their original format on the network, capturing a static image of the network and the associated traffic.

- *Protocol analyzer.* This tool captures and stores packet information, including consolidated statistical information for potential forensic analysis.

- *Traceroute and whois tools.* These tools can be helpful in tracing an intruder to the location of the source computer and allow IP address blocking and reporting.

▪ **Heartbeat signals** Communications traffic that signals the health of the building control system. It is also referred to as a *watchdog timer, keep-alive,* or *health status.*

Incident Categorization

Once positively identified, a cyber-physical attack should be categorized, and the response prioritized based on that categorization. Categorization should be based on the type of incident and the potential damage to the ICS (see Table 2-3).

Table 2-3. *Incident Categorization*

Event	Decision
BCS Network down	IT Tech Support and building maintenance team perform an assessment
Environmental problems (A/C, power, etc.)	Building maintenance team performs an assessment
Building unusable for 2 days or *less*	Building maintenance team and Incident Response Team (IRT) perform an assessment
Building unusable for *more* than 2 days	Activate Recovery Procedures
Building equipment is destroyed	Activate Recovery Procedures

Keep in mind that when a cyber-physical attack occurs at your building or installation, other cyber-physical attacks will be occurring at other buildings at the very same time. So, if you are relying on third-party maintenance service providers, bear in mind your phone call is only one of many they will receive. Recovery activity will be prioritized (see Table 2-4).

Table 2-4. *Incident Decision Points and Actions*

Decision Point	Actions				Category
1. Cyber "event" is discovered by IDS or unexpected equipment failure	2. Event is confirmed to be "Incident"	3. Recovery Procedures activated	4. Alarm sounds	5. Building evacuated	Initiation
	2. If no, then	3. Recovery Procedures is not activated	4. Return to normal operations	5. Evaluate response	Determination
6. Determine scope of incident and assess damage after building access is allowed	7. If small scope with no to minimal damage, then	8. Repair and begin clean up	9. Return to normal operations	10. Notify management and tenants of situation	Short Evacuation May Be Required
	7. Moderate to large scope or moderate to severe damage, then	8. Activate alternate site	9. Activate Incident Recovery Team	10. Notify management and tenants of situation	Moderate to Severe Damage to Building or Infrastructure

(continued)

Table 2-4. (*continued*)

Decision Point	Actions				Category
11. Assess damage	12. If damage is moderate and will be able to return in 30 days or less	13. Complete repairs as necessary while operating at alternate site	14. Return to building	15. Return to normal operations	Moderate Severe Damage to Building or Infrastructure
	12. If more than 30 days expected for repairs, locate to new building	13. Order supplies and equipment	14. Set up and operate at new facility while completing repairs	15. Return to normal operations	Severe Damage to Building or Infrastructure
	12. If total loss, locate to new facility	13. Rebuild	14. Set up at new facility while completing repairs	15. Return to normal operations	

Mitigation

Mitigation and segregation are needed to prevent the spread of malware to other buildings and installations not already affected. A hacker will leave lots of malware on your BCS, including the first malware that he installed—a callback routine that automatically tries to reconnect to the attack server if your system was disconnected or rebooted. Mitigation would block the intruder and deny him the opportunity to do further damage; allow maintenance personnel to carefully examine building equipment; restart the equipment manually; replace all BCS servers; and restore the BCS to normal operation. Additional information can be found in NIST SP 800-83, "Guide to Malware Incident Prevention and Handling," issued in November 2005.

Once you have established that a cyber-physical attack is underway, you have to rely on the building maintenance personnel to use their judgment and ability to act fast. Temporarily halting automatic services and shifting to manually operated equipment is a potentially disruptive measure, but it is the safe bet. Most building equipment is designed so it can be operated in manual mode and maintenance personnel should practice shifting to manual operation periodically. The desired goal is to mitigate the incident effectively with the least amount of loss in functionality. When the precursors for a cyber-physical attack are so obvious even a fifth-grader is aware, it's time to give up "connectedness" and go "off the grid." Do not wait until the nation goes to DEFCON 3.

Troubleshooting

Troubleshooting is a form of problem solving applied to repair failed equipment or systems. It is a logical, systematic search for the source of a problem so that it can be solved, and so the equipment or systems can be made operational again. In the case of a cyber-physical attack against building equipment or systems, the symptoms of a problem can have many possible causes. The problem is initially described as symptoms of malfunction, and troubleshooting is the process of determining and remedying the causes of these symptoms. Events or inputs to the system are expected to generate specific results or outputs. Any unexpected or undesirable behavior is a symptom. Simply replacing a failed piece of equipment, such as a pump or motor, would be futile without first containing the source of the problem—the *hacked* building control system.

Many building control systems can generate reports to help troubleshoot problems. If a problem is noted, it's important to look at all the original settings and any possible overrides on a piece of equipment to help determine the cause. Use of BCS energy management features— such as real-time monitoring of a building's energy-related data—may be helpful, but keep in mind this too can be "spoofed." So, the energy use information may appear perfectly normal when in fact energy use can be much higher than the BCS indicates.

Step 1: Confirm that the "event" is a Cyber-Physical Attack

When only one piece of equipment fails, it is probably not a cyber-physical attack. Depending on the conditions of failure, several pieces of equipment may fail because of their interdependencies. For example, if the commercial power to the building goes down, lots of things won't work. The air handling unit (AHU) fan motor stops pushing air into conditioned offices; the chillers shut down (unless they has backup power), office lights go out; and the elevators return to ground floor. This is all normal.

A cyber-physical attack is difficult to confirm. If the BCS is non-responsive (authorized users are locked out) or if BCS displays indicate that equipment is operating within normal parameters, but actual phenomenon contradicts the displays (such as rooms are inexplicably getting warmer), a cyber-physical attack may be underway. There is a strong likelihood that a cyber-physical attack is underway when multiple systems that are not dependent on each other begin to exhibit anomalous behavior. For example, if the building still has commercial power, but the cooling tower pumps and fans fail and the building elevators mysteriously go to the wrong floors or don't work at all, a cyber-physical attack may be underway. If the lights in office areas then begin to mysteriously turn off and on, and hot water heaters begin to produce 150-degree water (scalding hot), a cyber-physical attack is definitely underway. Once you've confirmed a cyber-physical attack is underway, if your BCS has an Internet connection (shame on you), *do not sever the connection immediately.* The hacker assumed your first response would be to sever the Internet connection, so there is a strong possibility that loss of Internet connectivity will automatically activate any additional virus already uploaded to the BCS initiating more equipment failures.

Step 2: Slow Down the Attack. Assume that the BCS is no Longer Under your Command

If the hacker has not already done this, maintenance personnel (two-man rule) should begin by going to the mechanical rooms and manually turning off equipment that is showing anomalous behavior (at the device)—*not using the BCS*. Maintenance personnel probably already tried using the BCS anyway. Personnel should then physically switch remaining equipment to manual mode (again, at the device itself), and unplug the BCS connector at the device. If you do not unplug the BCS connector at the device, the hacker will reset the device so he can regain control of it. If your BCS display is displaying false equipment settings, the hacker may not know immediately that personnel are slowly switching equipment to manual mode. If your BCS is connected to the Internet, physically unplug the Internet connection. The BCS is the hacker's eyes and ears into the building. Now the hacker knows for sure that you are on to him.

Step 3: Stop the Attack. Shut Down the BCS

The hacker installed a virus on computer servers and clients and even the equipment itself that has not been activated yet, and he was monitoring maintenance personnel activity. If all equipment is set to manual mode, that should prevent more damage. Shut down the BCS and there is nothing he can do.

■ **Kill chain**   Kill chain analysis illustrates the sequence of stages that the hacker must progress through successfully before achieving the desired objective; one mitigation can disrupt the chain and stop the cyber-attack. The stages are reconnaissance and staging, delivery and attack, exploitation, installation, and system compromise. A kill chain analysis describes the very structure of a cyber-intrusion and the corresponding model guides analysis to inform actionable cyber security intelligence. Through this model, defenders can develop resilient mitigations against intruders and prioritize investments in new defensive technology or processes. (Source: Lockheed Martin)

Step 4: Assess the Damage to Whatever Failed, but Assume that all Equipment was Hacked

Examine equipment that was malfunctioning to determine the extent of the damage. Equipment that did not fail should also be examined because a virus may have been loaded at the device that could then contaminate the BCS when it is restored.

Step 5: Replace Infected Servers and Repair Damaged Building Equipment

Personnel should continue to operate equipment in manual mode until the BCS network is clean of harmful programs. This can *only* be done by replacing *all* servers and client workstations and reinstalling BCS configuration files and applications software.

Step 6: Reload the BCS and Restart Automatic Operation

At this point, I assume that your BCS backup was not stored on the same network that the hacker just attacked. Restoring a backup from a drive located on the network that was attacked will simply reload contaminated software. The software must be reloaded from a Rescue CD in the Jump Kit or the vendor's *original disc only. All* passwords should be changed using rigorous password requirements. Unused software modules should be deleted (the fact that most people leave unused software modules loaded with their *default password unchanged* always amuses me). Unused ports should be closed, and so forth. User access and privileges should be revisited. By now, you know the drill.

JUMP KIT

A container that has the items necessary to respond to a cyber-physical attack to help mitigate the effects of delayed reactions. It contains the tools the Incident Response Teams will need to restore a system to its last fully mission-capable state. Knowing what the recovery point should be is the key to ensuring all known remnants of an attack have been removed from all components of the BCS. This means all hardware and software are configured in accordance with operational requirements, and checksums and hashes are in conformance with vendor specifications.

Jump kit contents:

- Incident notifications list: Document contact information for the Information Assurance Manager
- Document stakeholders who could be affected by a cyber-physical attack on BCS
- Established notification procedures with management or chain of command
- Universal serial bus (USB) drives, bootable USB (or LiveCD) with up-to-date anti-malware, and other software tools that can read and/or write to file system
- Laptop with anti-malware utilities and Internet access (for downloads)
- Computer and network tool kit to add components, hard drives, connectors, wire cables, etc.
- Hard disk duplicators with write-block capabilities to capture hard drive images
- Firewall access control lists
- Firewall hard disk image
- IDS rules
- IDS image
- Back up of firewall, router, and switch IOS
- Backup of PLC configurations and firmware
- Backup RTU software, database, and configurations
- Back up of all other computer assets to include HMI, Historian, and Database
- Network map of all expected connections to the BCS

CHAPTER 3

■ ■ ■

Prevent Hackers from Destroying a Boiler

A *boiler* is a closed pressure vessel in which water or other fluid (hydronic) is used to heat a building, while a *furnace* uses warm air. The heat is different, and the way that heat is circulated through the building is different (see Table 3-1). Once in your BCS, a hacker can send any one of many locking and blocking error codes to the boiler to shut it down. Interrupting the fuel that feeds the boiler or furnace or interfering with the combustion process is problematic at best, but a boiler that has a loss of feed water and is permitted to boil dry can be extremely dangerous. If feed water is then sent into that empty boiler, the small cascade of incoming water instantly boils on contact with the superheated metal shell and leads to a violent explosion that cannot be controlled even by steam safety valves.

Table 3-1. *BCS Interface to a Boiler or Furnace*

Supply water temperature

Flue gas temperature

Fuel pressure

Flame signal

Actual fuel throughput

Combustion efficiency

Gas fuel volume

O2 value

Unit pressure

Fault history

Total start-ups

Operating hours counter

Supply air condensing temperature

© Luis Ayala 2016
L. Ayala, *Cyber-Physical Attack Recovery Procedures*, DOI 10.1007/978-1-4842-2065-8_3

■ **Boiler lockout** There are two types of lockouts that a boiler may experience when a manual reset limit device trips (error code for low water, high or low pressure, flame failure, blocked flue, or low air). **Manual reset** lockouts require the operator press the reset button. **Automatic reset** lockouts self-reset when the error condition is cleared.

Boiler Explosion

Of course, building engineers assume none of this can happen because of the safety systems designed to prevent catastrophe. Keep in mind that Chernobyl had safety features that were turned off. A hacker will disable safety features without your knowledge. Failure to protect boilers from a cyber-physical attack can (and likely will) result in a catastrophe. The most common ways a hacker can "destroy a boiler" are listed in Table 3-2.

Table 3-2. *Cyber-Attack Tree: Ways that a Hacker Can Destroy a Boiler*

Fuel Explosion

Low Water Level

Improper Blowdown

Improper Warm-up

Pull a Vacuum on the Boiler

Flame Impingement

Overfiring

The most dangerous situation is a fuel explosion in a boiler or furnace. Conditions can be created for an explosion to occur by a hacker maliciously changing the configuration profile (the operating parameters) so the BCS "thinks" the boiler or furnace is operating properly when in fact it is exceeding manufacturer settings and no alarm would be sounded. A hacker can cause a boiler fuel explosion several ways:

- *Fuel-rich mixture*: A hacker can use the BCS to create high concentrations of unburned fuel by turning off the flame, overriding the automatic safety shutoff and allowing fuel flow to continue unabated. When the flame is restored, the unburned fuel ignites in a very rapid explosion. A fuel-rich mixture can also occur when insufficient air is supplied for the amount of fuel being burned. The hacker is then counting on maintenance personnel adding air with a fire in the unit, resulting in a huge explosion. Maintenance personnel should always trip the unit, purge thoroughly, and then correct the configuration profile.

- *Poor atomization of oil*: Accumulation of any unburned combustible fuel in the furnace can result in an explosion. Boilers have exploded because of poor atomization of oil, which results in incomplete combustion causing unburned oil puddling in the furnace. A hacker would increase the atomizing steam (or air) pressure and increase the fuel oil pressure far above the manufacturer's original settings.

- *Improper purge*: Explosions have happened after a combustion problem that caused a burner trip. A hacker can cause a flame failure. Maintenance personnel attempt to relight the burner without investigating the cause, and during multiple attempts to relight the burner, oil is sprayed into the furnace. The oil on the hot furnace floor releases combustible gases. When maintenance personnel relight the flame, they ignite the large amount of unburned combustible gases in the furnace, resulting in a huge explosion.

A catastrophe can be prevented by allowing the furnace to *purge thoroughly* before attempting to relight the flame. This is particularly important if fuel has spilled into the furnace. The purge will evacuate any unburned gases until the concentration is below explosive limits.

Hot Water Heater Explosion

Fire departments are familiar with the explosive potential of even a small hot-water heater. If a hacker can cause the hot-water heater tank (a pressure vessel) to flash into explosive failure at 332°F, the explosion will hurl burning building contents in all directions with tremendous force. Equipment several rooms from the point of the explosion become airborne and people in the mechanical room can be injured or killed as the pressure vessel explodes. It is important to remember that the blast from an explosion in a mechanical room travels through building ductwork. I have seen air vents on the other side of a building blown out from a blast event.

An example of the devastating power of a large pressure vessel explosion is the amphibious assault ship *USS Iwo Jima*. In October 1990, the *Iwo Jima* had been operating in the Persian Gulf for approximately two months and had developed some leaks in the ship's 600-psi steam propulsion plant.

A variety of maintenance items were planned, including overhauling the main steam valve that supplies steam to one of the ship's turbine-driven electrical generators. This valve would be considered a boiler-boundary stop valve. When the second turbine generator was started, the recently overhauled valve was opened to allow for steam at 600 psi and 850 degrees to pass. Within moments, the valve was leaking steam badly.

Before the captain could stop the ship, the bonnet completely blew off the valve and dumped steam from two large boilers into the boiler room. All ten of the crewmembers in the boiler room were killed. In this case, the cause of this catastrophic accident was the installation of nuts made of an improper material for the job. Increasing a building's boiler pressure above the maximum recommended by hacking into the BCS would achieve the same result.

■ **Boiler sequence controller hack** ˊ Boiler controller, burner programmer, burner controller, sequence controller, and programmable sequence controllers, measure the temperature of the combined water flow of a multi-boiler installation. They are pre-programmed for the automatic operation of gas/oil burners and they regulate the number of boilers operating to match the required demand. They continuously monitor the flame and can control how many boilers fire up at one time for safe start-up. They provide output for blower ignition solenoid valves with prefixed timing for continuous flame supervision. Hackers can turn all the boilers on full blast.

Low Water Conditions

Severe damage to a boiler will result under low water conditions because furnace temperatures typically exceed 1,800°F and the strength of steel decreases when higher than 800°F. The presence of water in all tubes of the furnace is the only thing that allows a boiler to withstand the high temperature. Low water conditions will cause steel boiler tubes to melt completely. A modern boiler is equipped with an automatic low-water switch that trips the burner and shut down the forced draft fan. This shuts down the heat input. If a hacker can defeat your boiler's low-water trip switch, *you will have an explosion.*

A hacker can create these low water conditions by any of the following actions: shutdown feedwater pump; shutdown control valve; loss of water to the deaerator or make-up water system; shutdown drum level controller; loss of plant air pressure to the control valve actuator; lifting the safety valve; and a large sudden change in steam demand.

Unfortunately, boilers equipped with low-water trips are destroyed every year because it is not uncommon for maintenance personnel to *disable trip circuits* to reduce nuisance trips. Installation of a self-monitoring device followed by automatic routine testing would allow two independent circuits to verify whether the measuring electrode is functioning properly. The first circuit would act as the primary alarm when low water is identified. A second circuit can be installed that is *totally independent of the BCS* to sense if there is a low water condition in the boiler, and if so, it will shut down the boiler safely.

Preventive Measures

The following practices should be followed to prevent hackers from destroying a boiler:

- Investigate and verify the cause of a trip before attempting to relight the boiler.

- Periodic observation of the burner flame to identify combustion problems.

- Before lighting a boiler, always purge the furnace thoroughly to evacuate the inventory of unburned gases. This is particularly important if oil has spilled into the furnace.

- Verify that the water treatment system is operating properly.

- *Never* disable a low water trip.

- Verify that the water leaving the deaerator is free of oxygen, that the deaerator is operated at the proper pressure, and that the storage tank water is at saturation temperature. A continuous vent from the deaerator is necessary to discharge non-condensable gases.

- Continuously monitor the quality of condensate coming back to enable the diversion of the condensate in the event of a catastrophic process equipment failure.

- Never blowdown a furnace wall header while the boiler is operating.

- The warm-up curve should be strictly followed (typically, do not increase the water temperature over 100°F per hour).

- Ensure that the steam drum vent valve is opened whenever the boiler pressure is less than 5 psig.

The following practices are recommended to prevent problems with poor water treatment:

- Verify boiler feedwater is sufficient for the temperatures and pressures involved.

- Verify water leaving the deaerator is free of oxygen, that the deaerator is operated at the proper pressure, and that the water is at saturation temperature for the pressure.

- The boiler should be inspected on a regular basis.

- The water side of the deaerator should be inspected on a regular basis because a deaerator can rupture and all the water in the deaerator would immediately flash to steam.

Improper Warm-up

If a hacker can access the BCS and change the configuration profile, he can cause severe equipment damage by accelerating the warm up of the boiler too quickly (more than 100°F per hour). Going through start-up, operation, and shutdown creates higher equipment stresses for any boiler than continuous operation at the maximum rated capacity.

Start-up Procedures

When a cyber-attack occurs, boilers should be shut down immediately and maintenance personnel should examine boilers carefully before returning them to service even under manual operation. Before a boiler is returned to service, boiler operators must check over the entire system and carefully review operating procedures.

Start-up Checks

Immediately prior to boiler start-up perform the following:

- Check that ventilation and combustion air openings are clean and free of debris.

- Verify water level.

- Check that stack dampers are open.

- Examine the furnace for foreign material.

- Check the furnace for fuel accumulation.

- Make sure that manual fuel valves are open.

Hackers may be able to create carbon monoxide in the mechanical rooms using the BCS. Carbon monoxide poisoning causes more fatalities and illnesses during one year than the failure of pressure vessels and combustion explosions. The two major reasons why generation of carbon monoxide occurs in the combustion process are: improper mixing of the combustion air with the fuel; and incomplete burning because of an inadequate supply of combustion air.

A good carbon monoxide indicator (if natural gas is used) is an unpleasant odor. If oil is the fuel, smoke or soot may be released, or the smell of unburned oil may be evident. The improper mixing of combustion air and fuel is most likely to occur because of the adjustment of certain components that comprise the burner. Given the fact that boilers have undergone rigorous development and testing programs, poor mixing is unlikely to be the result of a design deficiency. It is more likely to be the result of improper field adjustment or "hacker tinkering."

■ **Lockout/tagout (LOTO)**   Lock and tag is a safety procedure that is used in industry and research settings to ensure that dangerous machines are properly shut off and not able to be started up again prior to the completion of maintenance or servicing work. It requires that hazardous energy sources be "isolated and rendered inoperative" before work is started on the equipment in question. The isolated power sources are then locked and a tag is placed on the lock identifying the worker who has placed it. The worker then holds the key for the lock ensuring that only he or she can start the machine. This prevents accidental start-up of a machine while it is in a hazardous state or while a worker is in direct contact with it. Lockout/tagout is used across industries as a safe method of working on hazardous equipment and is mandated by law in some countries. (Source: Wikipedia)

CHAPTER 4

■ ■ ■

Prevent Hackers from Destroying a Pressure Vessel

Pressure vessels are designed to store a gas or liquid at a pressure substantially higher (10,000 psig) than the ambient pressure and are engineered with a safety factor, corrosion allowance, and minimum design temperature (for brittle fracture). A shell and tube heat exchanger is a type of pressure vessel commonly used in buildings. Pressure vessels are typically fitted with a mechanical safety valve or a relief valve to ensure that the design pressure is not exceeded in normal operation; however, the pressure differential is extremely dangerous, and fatal accidents have occurred in the past. Pressure vessels require sophisticated industrial controls to operate properly and this delicate balance is a potential vulnerability to a sophisticated cyber-physical attack by a determined hacker with engineering knowledge of the targeted equipment.

For example, auto-refrigeration is a phenomenon common to liquefied compressed gas. Liquefied compressed gases exist in both the liquid and gaseous phases at ambient temperatures with pressures ranging from 2 psig up to 2,500 psig. Withdrawal of propane gas from a tank reduces the temperature of the liquid propane and the tank itself with the temperature decreasing more as the gas withdrawal rate increases.

Withdrawing gas from a pressure vessel reduces the pressure as well as the temperature within the vessel. The gas that is withdrawn is replaced as the liquid vaporizes by absorbing heat from the remaining liquid and the vessel itself. Auto-refrigeration occurs when the gas is withdrawn at a rapid rate so that cooling exceeds the heat available from ambient sources. Auto-refrigeration of a pressure vessel not designed for low-temperature operation places the safety of the vessel in question because it could be cooled to temperatures at which vessel failure by brittle fracture may occur.

Microscopic flaws in the welds located in areas of high stress are subject to rapid crack growth when vessel temperatures reach the *nil ductility temperature* (the temperature at which the behavior of the vessel steel changes from ductile to brittle).

A determined hacker tinkering with the pressure vessel controls may be able to simply release the gas or liquid causing an environmental spill or worse, create a potentially dangerous event by taking advantage of a predisposing condition.

■ **Predisposing condition**   A condition that exists within an organization, a mission/business process, enterprise architecture, or information system including its environment of operation, which contributes to (i.e., increases or decreases) the likelihood that one or more threat events, once initiated, will result in undesirable consequences or adverse impact to organizational operations and assets, individuals, other organizations, or the nation. (Source: SP 800-30)

© Luis Ayala 2016

L. Ayala, *Cyber-Physical Attack Recovery Procedures*, DOI 10.1007/978-1-4842-2065-8_4

Pressure vessels are a special class of equipment that should be segregated from the rest of the building control system in a separate enclave.

■ **Blowdown stack hack**   A chimney or vertical stack that is used in an emergency to vent the pressure of components of a chemical, refinery, or other process. The purpose is to prevent loss of containment of volatile liquids and gases. Hacking the controls of a blowdown stack could cause pressure to build up. The failure of the blowdown stack to contain vented hydrocarbons led to a catastrophic explosion at a BP refinery in Texas City in 2005.

CHAPTER 5

■ ■ ■

Prevent Hackers from Destroying Chillers

Chillers are not as dangerous as steam boilers or pressure vessels, but a hacker can wreak havoc with your chillers if he knows what he's doing. The old absorption chillers generated hydrogen gas naturally as a result of the reaction of lithium bromide with the steel surfaces of chiller, but they are not very common anymore. A hacker attempting to disrupt the chilled water system will generally mess with the refrigerant flow or the condenser water temperature. If a hacker can cause the pressure differential (lift) to exceed the capacity of the compressor, the backward pressure flow causes the chiller to surge. Conversely, if the hacker can cause the pressure in the evaporator to drop, that can also cause the compressor to surge. If the compressor surges, you'll know because it is very noisy.

The cooling tower can also cause the compressor to surge with reduction in the flow of water to the condenser. If the cooling tower fan stops, you will get a high temperature condition. Of course, the hacker would have to defeat the low temperature safety switch, so it does not shut down the chiller automatically. Chiller surge causes damage to the rotating assemblies. When a second or lag machine must be started, the timing of the isolation valves is crucial in preventing a surge condition. If the valve does not open after 90 seconds, the lag system automatically shuts back down in a failure mode.

■ **Rupture disc**   A non-reclosing pressure relief device that typically protects a pressure vessel, equipment, or system from over pressurization or potentially damaging vacuum conditions, also known as a *pressure safety disc*, a *burst disc*, a *bursting disc*, or a *burst diaphragm*.

If a hacker shuts down the chiller and leaves the pump on, the water in the system heats up increasing the pressure on the cooling side of the chiller. That will increase the pressure in the chamber causing the rupture disc to fail, releasing the refrigerant into the atmosphere. If the refrigerant is R-11, maintenance personnel can be overcome and being unable to breathe possibly pass out from lack of oxygen. This is not the case with R-34 refrigerant. Of course, repairing the rupture disc and replacing lost refrigerant takes time. You should be back up and running in a couple days (provided you have a preferred maintenance agreement with the vendor). That is unless, of course, there were 600,000 buildings attacked simultaneously.

© Luis Ayala 2016

L. Ayala, *Cyber-Physical Attack Recovery Procedures*, DOI 10.1007/978-1-4842-2065-8_5

Troubleshooting Chillers

Begin by looking for indicators or codes that come up on the diagnostic readouts.

Make a visual inspection of the electrical panel, water piping, and pump tank system. Look for obvious problems such as burned or broken wires, water pump not running, water valves shut off, and improper system water temperature.

- Is the chiller running and not cooling, or not running at all?

- Is the pump circulating water? What is the water temperature?

- If the chiller isn't running, check the high voltage circuits.

- Does the chiller have power? Check all the fuses.

- Start at the power side of the control transformer and check wire by wire.

- Trace the power wire from safety to safety.

- Check the water flow switch and the freezestat control.

- Strap temperature probes on the suction, discharge, and liquid lines.

- Watch all the pressures, temperatures, and amperages.

Chiller Cyber-Attack Tree

The following are some simple hacks that the attacker may use:

- *Low-pressure trip*: BCS thinks that the refrigerant is low; has low or no water flow; or has a clogged water filter or screen.

- *High-pressure trip*: BCS thinks that the water-cooled condenser has poor or no flow; the air-cooled condenser is blocked with debris or has a fan not working; or that the chilled water tank temperature is too high.

- *Oil failure trip*: BCS thinks that there is either low superheat or low oil.

- *Freezestat*: BCS thinks that there is poor water flow or that the thermostat is set too low.

- *Blown fuses or starter trips*: BCS thinks that there is an over-amped motor, compressor, or wires.

- *System not reaching thermostat setpoint*: BCS thinks that the evaporator is iced up.

- *Proof of flow*: BCS thinks that the flow or pressure switches in water circuit are suffering from low or no flow, or that the water filter is blocked or the water valve is shut off.

■ ■ ■

CHAPTER 6

Prevent Hackers from Destroying a Gas Fuel Train

A fuel train is a specially designed series of pipes, valves, regulators, and switches located in the mechanical room, supplying pressurized fuel to industrial burners. A typical fuel train has several components, each with a specific purpose. The manual shut-off valve (MSOV) is used to shut off the fuel supply for maintenance. A gas pressure regulator valve (PRV) maintains the fuel at a constant pressure. A low-pressure gas switch equipped with a safety lockout senses when gas pressure is too low for the burner to operate properly. This tells the operator to check the gas pressure, since the burner will not try to restart until the switch is reset.

Safety shut-off valves (SSOV) automatically open and shut off the fuel supply to the burner. The vent valve is normally an open valve and energizes to close. Whenever the SSOV is closed, the vent valve is open, so if any gas is leaking it will vent to the atmosphere.

A high gas pressure switch is installed to shut down the burner before an unsafe condition can occur. This switch is equipped with a safety lockout that tells the operator that the gas regulator failed since the burner will not restart until the switch is manually reset. A firing rate valve equipped with a modulating motor controlled by boiler pressure or temperature regulates the amount of fuel to the burner and controls the air damper.

A hacker would seek to defeat the safety features and allow gas pressure to build up and exceed the design limits of the fuel train. This may be possible if the SSOVs are prevented from shutting off the fuel supply in a high gas pressure situation. The SSOV would need to remain open to prevent the vent valve from being vented. Alternatively, if the SSOV is allowed to open and close quickly, vented gas would fill the mechanical room where the boiler is located resulting in spontaneous combustion.

© Luis Ayala 2016
L. Ayala, *Cyber-Physical Attack Recovery Procedures*, DOI 10.1007/978-1-4842-2065-8_6

CHAPTER 7

■ ■ ■

Prevent Hackers from Destroying a Cooling Tower

A cooling tower is used to dispose of unwanted heat from a chiller. Water-cooled chillers operating on the principle of evaporative cooling are normally more energy-efficient than air-cooled chillers. To achieve better performance (more cooling), they are designed to increase the surface area and the time of contact between the air and water flow. A "collection basin" is used to collect and contain the cooled water after its interaction with the airflow. Make-up water is added to the system to compensate for water lost due to evaporation.

Cooling tower water is filtered to remove particulates and treated with biocides and algaecides to prevent growths that could interfere with the continuous flow of the water and prevent the growth of Legionella, including species that cause legionellosis or Legionnaires' disease, most notably L. pneumophila, or Mycobacterium avium. Cooling towers are fitted with electrical immersion heaters, steam coils, or hot-water coils in the collection basin to prevent freezing. Obviously, the basin heater should not be operating in the summer, because that would contribute to growth of opportunistic pathogens.

Modern cooling towers are designed with a drift eliminator that provides multiple directional changes of airflow to prevent the escape of water droplets. They are designed to prevent excessively high water levels and possible overflow of the cold-water basin due to over pumping, clogged strainers, or makeup valve malfunction.

A hacker wishing to disrupt a building HVAC may decide to flood the cooling tower collection basin, turn off the fans and heat the water in the basin. Turning off the pumps or intermittent fan reversal would also cause damage to the cooling tower, chillers, or both. Another hack would be to search the installation files to determine the resonant operation speed of the unit that may result in vibrations, which could damage the components or structure, and/or create objectionable noise. The resonant speed ranges are identified at start-up and typically locked out to prevent the variable frequency drive to operate the motor at these resonant speeds. A hacker may also interfere with the chemical "pot" feeder that injects diluted liquid biocides directly to the collection water basin.

Another possible hack would be to spoof the *vibration cutout switch* (VCOS) to shut down the cooling tower. A VCOS is designed to cause a trip condition when it detects any vibration after a time delay. A VCOS can be mechanical or electronic, with a single setpoint containing one trip limit for alarm or shut down.

Troubleshooting Cooling Towers

Building maintenance personnel should disassemble screens and access panels for inspection; inspect the tower fill, support structure, sump and spray nozzles, fill valve, gear box, drive coupling, fan blades, and motor bearings; inspect wiring; check motor starter contacts for proper operation; megger test the motor and check the condition of the sump heater and contactor.

© Luis Ayala 2016
L. Ayala, *Cyber-Physical Attack Recovery Procedures*, DOI 10.1007/978-1-4842-2065-8_7

CHAPTER 8

■ ■ ■

Prevent Hackers from Destroying a Backup Generator

In 2007, CNN broadcast a demonstration of an "Aurora" cyber-physical attack of a 2.25 MW generator connected to a substation. This test was conducted at the Idaho National Laboratory (INL) for the Department of Homeland Security. INL staff injected a virus consisting of 20 lines of code that caused an out-of-phase condition that can damage alternating current (AC) equipment connected to the power grid.

■ **Aurora vulnerability hack**   In 2007, the Idaho National Laboratory (INL) conducted a test to demonstrate how a cyber-physical attack could destroy physical components of the electric grid. INL used a computer program to rapidly open and close a diesel generator's circuit breakers out of phase from the rest of the grid. Every time the breakers were closed, the torque from the synchronization caused the generator to bounce and shake, eventually causing parts of the generator to be ripped apart and sent flying as far as 80 feet. This vulnerability can be mitigated by preventing out-of-phase opening and closing of the circuit breakers. A cyber-physical attack that takes down a commercial power grid causes a rise in mortality rates as health and safety systems fail, a drop in trade as ports shut down, and disruption to transportation and infrastructure.

Connecting AC equipment out of phase is a known vulnerability, but doing it maliciously was brought to light by the test conducted by INL. This condition occurs when a circuit breaker or breakers are opened and closed rapidly, resulting in an out-of-phase condition. The test demonstrated the threat associated with rapidly disconnecting and reconnecting a generator to the grid, but out-of-phase, via physical or cyber intrusion of control systems conducted maliciously or unintentionally.

Because an Aurora event consists of the out-of-sync reconnecting of three-phase rotating equipment, just about any three-phase equipment (motors, generators) in manufacturing facilities, pipelines, refineries, electrified mass transit, data centers, and power plants can be attacked.

Risk mitigation is achieved by placing a hardware device that monitors for the rapid out-of-phase condition associated with an AUORA event between each substation and its loads. The device isolates the substation from its loads before the torque of the grid can be applied to the equipment. Two relay protection suppliers provide a Digital Protection and Control Devices (DPCD) capable of closing breakers that can adversely impact critical electrical rotating equipment: Cooper Power Systems, and Schweitzer Engineering Laboratories. They are relatively inexpensive and have wiring configurations similar to other relays.

© Luis Ayala 2016
L. Ayala, *Cyber-Physical Attack Recovery Procedures*, DOI 10.1007/978-1-4842-2065-8_8

■ **Power outage**   A short- or long-term loss of the electric power to an area (also called a *power cut*, a *power blackout*, a *power failure*, or a *blackout*). Power outages are categorized relating to the duration and effect of the outage:

- A **permanent fault** is a massive loss of power typically caused by a fault on a power line. Power is automatically restored once the fault is cleared.

- A **brownout** is a drop in voltage in an electrical power supply. The term *brownout* comes from the dimming experienced by lighting when the voltage sags. Brownouts can cause poor performance of equipment or even incorrect operation.

- A **blackout** is the total loss of power to an area and is the most severe form of power outage that can occur. Blackouts that result from or result in power stations tripping are particularly difficult to recover from quickly. Outages may last from a few minutes to a few weeks, depending on the nature of the blackout and the configuration of the electrical network.

CHAPTER 9

■ ■ ■

Prevent Hackers from Destroying Switchgear

Many large industrial facilities can have downtime costs of more than one million dollars per day. Equipment replacement times can easily be months. The risk should be obvious.

Historically, the only possible way to compromise electro-mechanical relays on some utilities' systems required physical access to the relay (For some reason, transformers are the target of choice for some snipers in California.) Unfortunately, the same digital control systems that enable these systems to be more operator-friendly and functional are turning these features into vulnerabilities. That's why it is so important to air-gap your controls so that an adversary cannot change any configuration parameters.

If a hacker can get into the BCS and cause devices to exceed the design amperage (such as load up a 1200 amp breaker), that would overload the wires and a flame would spread quickly throughout the switchgear. Then again, if an attacker can get into a manhole, he may be able to cause an arc fault and trigger an electrical fire. Of course, this is extremely dangerous and unless he knows what he is doing, he probably would not survive the attempt.

Overcurrent devices should be cleaned and lubricated as required; fusible switch units should be checked to make sure all fuses within the unit are from the same manufacturer and are of the same class and rating. Arcing failures will occur where connections have been loosened.

It may sound overly simplistic but once an adversary gets into your BCS, he can send the same commands to your equipment that your building maintenance personnel can send (see Table 9-1). An adversary can turn things on or off, cause equipment to shut down automatically when a certain trigger is activated, or cause pieces of equipment to work against each other. Imagine two fans at opposite ends of a length of ductwork, each blowing air toward the other fan.

Table 9-1. *Cyber-Attack Tree: Ways a Hacker Can Destroy an Electrical Switchgear*

Send invalid disconnect messages to meters.

Compromised head end.

Blocked DR messages.

Improper DRAS configuration causes inappropriate DR messages.

Spurious trip parameters added trips unit offline.

Equipment tripped offline through vendor remote connection.

Improper firewall rule configuration allows direct access from another network.

(continued)

© Luis Ayala 2016

L. Ayala, *Cyber-Physical Attack Recovery Procedures*, DOI 10.1007/978-1-4842-2065-8_9

Table 9-1. (*continued*)

Adversary sends DR message that causes services to send "last gasp" or "self-test failed" messages direct to devices.

Meter reconfigured via optical port.

Flood communications channel with other messages prevent legitimate DR messages from being received and transmitted.

Modify DRAS configuration to send DR messages at incorrect times or to incorrect devices.

Manufacture an artificial cascade to trigger blackout through sequential tripping of select feeders and components causing automated tripping due to power and voltage fluctuations.

Stop flow of wireless communications between devices.

Overwhelm alarm-processing capability by sending unnecessary alarms.

CHAPTER 10

■ ■ ■

Eight Steps to Defending Building Control System

I am including this list of recommendations in the hopes that readers will take action to protect their networks. If you only do these eight things, I estimate that you will reduce your vulnerability by 90 percent.

Discontinue Remote Connections to the BCS

Granted, the building maintenance personnel and equipment vendors want to access the equipment from the comfort of their recliner at home. So does the hacker. I have yet to see a BCS that does *not* have remote access. I asked an engineer once if his building had remote access. He said "No." I asked to see his network diagram. I pointed to a box on the diagram labeled "Modem." "What's this?" I asked. He replied, "Oh, that's only used by the vendor for diagnostics." Obviously, we had it removed.

Implement Application Whitelisting

Application whitelisting can *detect* and *prevent* malware from executing. Building control systems are typically static systems that rarely change so they are ideal for this defense. Application whitelisting is more effective than antivirus software because antivirus is not 100-percent effective.

■ **Application whitelist**　A list or register of entities that are being provided a particular privilege, service, mobility, access, or recognition. Entities on the list will be accepted, approved, and/or recognized. Whitelisting is the reverse of blacklisting, the practice of identifying entities that are denied, unrecognized, or ostracized.

Systematic Patch Management Regimen

Just like burglars look for unlocked doors, hackers look for unpatched systems. Start with an asset inventory and baseline to track needed patches. Ensure software patches are imported from a safe, known source (hackers have been known to create a "watering hole" website so unsuspecting maintenance staff could download an infected version of the patch) and the patch is implemented quickly upon release. Don't forget to scan and patch PC-based laptops used to patch the BCS. Only known-good company laptops should connect to the BCS for patching and these should be stored securely on site at all times.

© Luis Ayala 2016

L. Ayala, *Cyber-Physical Attack Recovery Procedures*, DOI 10.1007/978-1-4842-2065-8_10

Reduce the Attack Surface

The BCS should not connect to any other networks, especially the Internet. Lock down all unused ports. Turn off all unused services. Only allow real-time connectivity to external networks if there is a legitimate requirement. If one-way communication can accomplish a task, use optical separation ("data diode"). If bidirectional communication is necessary, then use a single open port over a restricted network path.

Build a Defendable Network Environment

Segment networks into logical enclaves and restrict host-to-host communications paths. This prevents hackers from expanding their access, while allowing normal system communications. Enclaving limits possible spread of malware and makes incident cleanup much faster and less costly. Consider using approved media instead of a network connection when transferring data from a secure network to a less secure network.

Manage Authentication

Hackers are increasing attempting to obtain legitimate credentials, especially those with highly privileged accounts, allowing them to masquerade as legitimate users. Implement three-factor authentication where possible. Reduce privileges to only what's needed. Implement secure passwords (14 characters) for all accounts and change all passwords at least every 90 days. Require separate credentials for separate networks and zones.

Monitor and Respond

Watch IP traffic for abnormal or suspicious communication. Watch IP traffic within the BCS network for malicious connections or content. Use host-based products to detect malicious software. Use login analysis (time and place for example) to detect stolen credential usage or improper access, verifying all anomalies with a quick phone call. Watch account/user administration actions to detect control manipulation.

Do Not Use BCS Workstations for Anything Else

Resist the temptation to use the BCS workstation for any other purpose. Do not allow connection of a BCS client computer to check email, download software updates, surf the Web, or play computer games. The BCS workstation should not even be connected to the enterprise network. That's how "they" get in. Exercise good cyber-hygiene.

CHAPTER 11

■ ■ ■

Block Hacker Surveillance of Your Buildings

So far, I've discussed the ability of an adversary to cause physical damage to your facilities, but there is another aspect to their activities that needs attention. The fact is that hackers are monitoring your company activities using *your* building control system and other building-related systems that your IT staff and security staff are probably completely unaware even exist.

Historically, IT staff has kept away from the building controls network, and for very good reasons. First of all, they don't know diddly about the building equipment being monitored. Secondly, they are not funded to get involved in facilities equipment—and the facilities folks don't want them involved either.

The security office is probably totally unaware the facilities folks have a direct digital controlled network that can be used by adversaries to monitor activities in your buildings in real time. They too are not familiar with the equipment or the capability of the equipment for misuse as an intelligence collection platform. The fact that they are not funded and don't have the training to ensure the security of these building control systems is another matter altogether.

Basically, the three most important groups needed to ensure the adversary is unable to penetrate your building controls aren't even talking to each other. When all heck breaks loose, they will be content to point the finger at each other and say it was the other guy's responsibility. In reality, no one is responsible and adversaries depend on the confusion to gain a foothold into your day-to-day activities.

Case in point, not long ago it was discovered that someone in China was listening in on confidential conversations about trade negotiations at the U.S. Chamber of Commerce. It was only after network printers at the Chamber of Commerce began spewing out documents written in Chinese that an investigation revealed the thermostats in a conference room were retasked remotely to act like microphones and the conversations were transmitted over the building controls network around the world where they were recorded by the hackers.

Is this an isolated incident? Probably not. Can industrial spies listen into conversations in your CEO's office? Is there a thermostat in the room? Is it made in China? Is your building controls network connected to the Internet? Do the math.

Another source of information about your company is the Computerized Maintenance Management System that the facilities office uses to track equipment maintenance, preventive maintenance, and repair work orders. The facilities staff typically walks around the building with handheld wireless tablets that tell them what equipment needs filters replaced for example and when. These wireless devices are easily hacked. Your adversary tracks the information and knows who your maintenance people are, when they are out on vacation, their phone number and email (home and office), their work hours, the equipment that has broken down and when it happened, whether repair parts are in the warehouse and where, and on and on. You would not believe the amount of information an adversary can extract from a CMMS. Yet the CMMS is

© Luis Ayala 2016
L. Ayala, *Cyber-Physical Attack Recovery Procedures*, DOI 10.1007/978-1-4842-2065-8_11

sometimes the least secure IT platform in your entire operation. Some of the CMMS systems include a list of passwords that staff uses to get into the BCS, change configurations, and so forth. Some also reveal who has administrator privileges. That can be one very leaky boat.

The good news is that as long as the adversary is more interested in listening in on your "confidential" conversations, the less likely he is to try and blow up your equipment. The bad news is that the day will come when he is less interested in listening in and more interested in doing real damage to your factory and offices.

The best way to prevent use of the BCS for surveillance of your building is to read Chapter 10 and do what it says. When the adversary that was able to get into your BCS decides to shut down your building, you will not be able to stop him from doing some damage. Preventing him from getting into your BCS is the best strategy.

CHAPTER 12

■ ■ ■

Cyber-Physical Attack Recovery Procedures Template

■ **Note**   A soft copy of these forms (fully editable with fillable fields) is available for download at www.apress.com/9781484220641.

<<Company Name>>
<<Facility Name>>
<<Date>>

The Cyber-Physical Attack Recovery Procedures provide guidance when responding to a cyber-attack on the Building Control System and documenting the nature and scope of the cyber-attack. The Recovery Procedures Template consists of **checklists** and **functional performance tests** to assist the Incident Response Team in restoring normal building operations in a pre-determined sequence, based on mission prioritization.

One checklist shall be filled out specifically for each piece of equipment (e.g., AHU-1, AHU-2, AHU-3, etc.) and the functional performance tests include normal operating parameters (e.g., 40 psig, 40°F to 95°F) based on information collected during initial installation and/or during equipment commissioning, for comparison with current readings. Some checklists require you to attach drawings indicating the location of important switches, valves and gauges to be checked, as well as equipment shutdown and start-up, and Sequence of Operation instructions. Checklists may also list dependencies and related functions that make up the service such as water and power; how those dependencies interrelate; and the tools, procedures, and personnel necessary to restore the particular equipment or service to normal operation.

The following flow chart should give you a general idea of the recovery process.

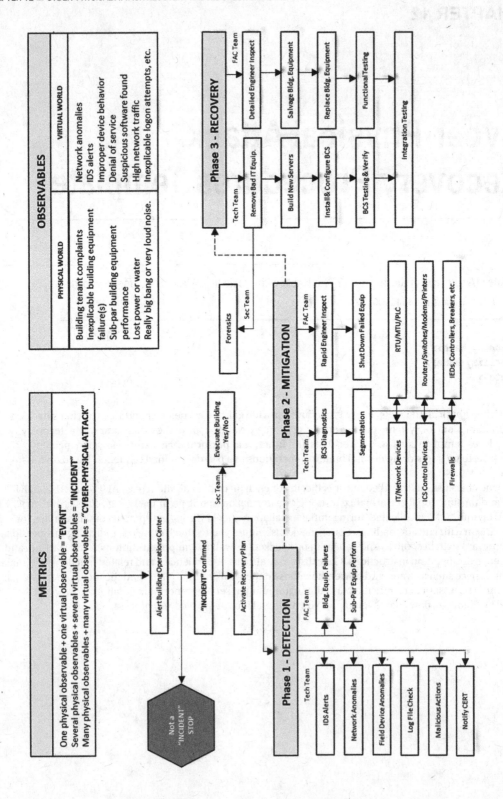

START HERE

These are the steps taken when a cyber-physical event occurs. The person who discovers the event will call the Building Operations Office. The sources should be provided with a contact procedure and contact list. Sources requiring contact information may be:

Person Discovering the Event Should Call:	
Contact	**Telephone Number**
Helpdesk	
Building Operations Office	
Security Office	
IT Support Office	
Whichever office is contacted first shall contact the other offices.	

■ **Note**   Enter telephone numbers and post this information where staff can see it.

The Office Alerted of the Event will Log:	
Name of the caller	
Time of the call	
Contact information about the caller	
Caller physical location	
The nature of the event	
How was the event detected?	
What equipment or persons were involved?	
Location of equipment or persons involved	

The facilities office staff member who receives the call will contact the Recovery Procedures Coordinator using email *and* phone messages while certain that other appropriate backup personnel and designated managers are contacted.

The Incident Response Team will meet and determine a response strategy.

The Staff Member Could Possibly add the Following:	
Is the affected equipment mission-critical?	
What is the severity of the potential impact?	
Name of equipment being targeted, along with operating system, IP address, and location.	
IP address and any information about the origin of the attack.	

Incident Response Team Initial Meeting/Discussion	
Is the event real or perceived?	
Is the event still in progress?	
What equipment or system is threatened and how critical is it?	
What is the impact on the building should the attack succeed? Minimal, serious, or critical?	
Where is the equipment located physically and on the BCS network?	
Is the event inside the trusted network?	
Is the response urgent?	
Can the event be quickly contained?	
Will the response alert the attacker and do we care?	
What type of event is this? (virus, worm, intrusion, abuse, damage)	

■ **Note**   Create a new event ticket for each call. There will be many.

EVENT TICKET

Work Order #:	Government Work Order #:
Work Order Type:	Customer Ref #:
Report Date:	Work Order Status:
Building:	Asset Worked On:

Additional Location Information:

Customer Request:

Conditions Found:

Actions Taken:

	Status:			Date:	
Date:	Technician Name	Start Time	Stop Time	Regular Hours	OT Hours

Part #	Description		Quantity	Unit Cost	Total Cost
Supply Rep Name		Technician Name/ Date Received		Supervisor Approval for High Value Items	

Customer Signature & Date Completed	Customer Rating
Technician Signature & Date Completed	Customer Comment
QC Inspector Signature & Date Completed	QC Comment

Event Category. Event will be categorized into the highest applicable level of one of the following categories (pick one):

Event Category	Description
One	A threat to life, safety, or the public
Two	A threat to sensitive buildings or utilities
Three	A threat to computer systems
Four	A disruption of building mission or services

INCIDENT RESPONSE TEAM

Incident Response Team members will use the checklists and perform the functional performance tests specified herein in the order specified in the Equipment Restoration Priority List. IRT members sign off after each test. Incident Response Team members will establish and follow one of the following procedures basing their response on the incident assessment:

- Worm response procedure

- Virus response procedure

- System failure procedure

- Active intrusion response procedure: Is critical data at risk?

- Inactive Intrusion response procedure

- System abuse procedure

- Property theft response procedure

- Website denial of service response procedure

- Database or file denial of service response procedure

- Spyware response procedure

■ **Note**   The Incident Response Team may create additional procedures, which are not foreseen in this document. If there is no applicable procedure in place, the team must document what was done and later establish a procedure for the incident.

Incident Response Team members will use forensic techniques, including reviewing system logs, looking for gaps in logs, reviewing intrusion detection logs, and interviewing witnesses and the incident victim to determine how the incident was caused. Only authorized personnel should be performing interviews or examining evidence, and the authorized personnel may vary by situation and the organization.

Upon management approval, the changes will be implemented.

Incident Response Team members will restore the affected building control system(s) to the uninfected state. They may do any or more of the following:

- Reinstall the affected building control system(s) from scratch and restore data from backups if necessary. Preserve evidence before doing this.

- Make *all* users change *all* passwords.

- Be sure that the building control system has been hardened by turning off or uninstalling unused services.

- Be sure that the building control system is fully patched.

- Be sure that real-time virus protection and intrusion detection is running.

- Be sure that the building control system is logging the correct events and to the proper level.

Documentation

The following shall be documented:

- How the incident was discovered.
- The category of the incident.
- How the incident occurred, whether through email, firewall, and so forth.
- Where the attack came from, such as IP addresses and other related information.
- What the recovery plan was.
- What was done in response?
- Whether the recovery procedures were effective.

Evidence Preservation

Make copies of logs, email, and other communication. Keep lists of witnesses. Keep evidence as long as necessary to complete prosecution and beyond in case of an appeal.

Notify Proper External Agencies

Notify the police and other appropriate agencies if prosecution of the intruder is possible. Add contact numbers here.

Notify Proper External Agencies

Agency	Contact
US Department of Homeland Security	877-776-7585 ICS-CERT@HQ.DHS.GOV
FBI – Cyber Division – CyWatch	855-292-3937 TCIU@IC.FBI.GOV
National Security Agency (Industry) (Government)	410-854-6091 BAO@NSA.GOV 410-854-4200 IAD_CCC@NSA.GOV
Police	

Assess Damages and Cost

Assess the damage to the organization and estimate both the equipment cost and the cost of the mitigation efforts.

INCIDENT RESPONSE TEAM MEMBER LISTING

Team Member Name	Cell Phone	Telephone	Time Called	Email
Management Team				
Leader				
Facilities Team				
Leader				
Tech Support Team				
Leader				
Security Team				
Leader				

■ **Note**   This list should be completed and kept current.

EQUIPMENT RECOVERY PRIORITY LIST

Equipment Recovery Priority List	
Priority	Description
1	
2	
3	
4	
5	
6	

■ **Note**   This list should be completed and kept current.

BCS NOTIFICATIONS REPORT

The following is a list of announced system vulnerabilities for the BCS network.

Announced BCS Vulnerabilities

Bulletin ID or Name	Description	System Affected	Release Date	Resolved	Impact

PATCH MANAGEMENT REPORT

The following is a list of installed and missing service packs on the BCS network.

Installed and Missing Service Packs

Bulletin ID or Name	Description	System Affected	Release Date	Severity	Lab Test Date	Patch Date	Complete Pending	Name of Tester

VULNERABILITY ASSESSMENTS HISTORY

The following are the types of internal and external vulnerability tests.

White-Box Test Team

This test team has complete access to the BCS network, including network diagrams, hardware, operating system, and application details. Knowledge of the network allows targeting specific building equipment, applications, and field devices.

Grey-Box Test Team

This test team simulates attack by a disgruntled employee. The test team has user level privileges and access permitted to the BCS network with certain security policies relaxed.

Black-Box Test Team

This test team has no prior knowledge of the BCS network (except possibly a website URL or IP address). The test team attempts to break into the BCS network remotely.

Scan Date	Testing Team & Type	Company	Recommendations

The following are vulnerability test types:

- **External Vulnerability Scan**: Identify network-facing vulnerabilities (monthly).

- **Internal Vulnerability Scan**: Identify network-facing vulnerabilities (quarterly).

- **External Vulnerability Assessment**: Identify configuration and architecture vulnerabilities (annual).

- **Internal Vulnerability Assessment**: Identify network, client, configuration, and physical vulnerabilities (annual).

- **Penetration Test**: Exploit any vulnerability to obtain access to building controls (annual).

PHASE 1: DETECTION

Observables

Historically, the primary reason many cyber-attacks went undetected for days, months, or years is because most cyber-attacks steal information. In the past, cyber-attacks targeted an enterprise's use of cyberspace for the purpose of disrupting, disabling, destroying, or maliciously controlling a computing environment/infrastructure; or destroying the integrity of the data or stealing controlled information. A cyber-physical attack on the other hand is a coordinated attack on vulnerable physical systems, making it much more difficult to conceal.

When anomalous behavior is observed such as multiple equipment failures, Intrusion Detection System alerts are sounded, or a catastrophic event occurs, the Incident Response Teams consult the **Event Diagnostics Table** to determine if the "event" is a possible cyber-physical attack. Incident Response Teams then consult the **BCS Integrity Checks** table to verify if a cyber-physical attack is underway. Incident Response Teams provide management with the facts necessary to make informed decisions regarding subsequent resumption and recovery activity.

Real-World Alerts

As building managers, we are constantly monitoring building equipment in the physical world looking for clues that something is amiss. Problems like the inability of the HVAC to maintain building temperature at a comfortable level, or smoke billowing from a mechanical room are what I call "observables." We actually *see, hear, or smell* that something is wrong in *the real world*. Sometimes it's the complaints from a building's occupants that tell us that something is wrong. We rely on electronic equipment to quickly detect observables in the real world. Things like automatic smoke detectors and fire alarms quickly point out serious problems because they are located throughout buildings.

The following are some observable events that tell us that something is wrong in the *real world*:

- Smoke
- Fire
- Leaks
- Smells
- Sounds
- Flashing red lights
- Multiple or frequent building occupant complaints
- Rooms too hot
- Rooms too cold
- Excessive energy use
- Equipment won't turn on
- Equipment won't turn off
- Explosions
- People passing out
- People vomiting

You get the idea.

Virtual-World Alerts

Observable events that tell us something is wrong in the *virtual world* include the following:

- No disk space or significantly reduced free disk space
- Unusually high CPU usage
- Unauthorized creation of new user accounts
- Attempted or actual use of administrator-level accounts
- Locked-out accounts
- Accounts in use when the user is not at work
- Cleared log files
- Full log files with an unusually large number of events
- Disabled antivirus software and other security controls
- Unexpected patch changes
- Requests for information about the system (social engineering attempts)
- Unexpected system or building equipment shutdown
- Stoppage or displayed error messages on a web, database, or application server
- Filenames containing unusual characters or new or unexpected files and directories
- Auditing configuration changes logged on the host records, especially the disabling of audit functionality
- A large number of bounced emails with suspicious content
- Unusual deviation from typical network traffic flows
- Erratic equipment behavior, especially when more than one device exhibits the same behavior
- Any apparent override of safety, backup, or failover systems
- Equipment, servers, or network traffic that has bursts of temporary high usage when the operational process itself is steady and predictable
- Unknown or unusual traffic from corporate or other network external to control systems network
- Unknown or unexpected firmware pulls or pushes
- Evidence of cyber-attack precursors, such as active port scanning or account harvesting
- Unusual patterns of communication gathering technical or security information
- Phishing attacks
- Information about the BCS is exfiltrated or leaked
- Denial-of-service attack

- Data, file system, software, or packets were altered
- Equipment configuration setpoints were altered at rest or in transit
- Unauthorized use of the BCS

Intrusion Detection System Alerts

Now, we also have to discover when something is going wrong in the "virtual world." We do this by installing an intrusion detection system (IDS). An IDS is a hardware or software product that gathers and analyzes information from various areas within a building control system to identify possible security breaches, which include both intrusions (attacks from outside the organizations) and misuse (attacks from within the organizations.)

An IDS alerts us whenever it detects suspicious behavior, such as any of these events:

- Unauthorized user logging in
- Virus or Trojan horse detected
- Rapid and/or continuous log-ins/log-outs
- Users logging into accounts outside of normal working hours
- Numerous failed login attempts
- User accounts attempting to escalate account privileges
- Suspicious software and/or configurations on a server or workstation
- Unusual system behavior
- Irregular process found
- Spontaneous reboots or screensaver change
- Unusually slow performance or usually active CPU
- CPU cycles up and cycles down for no apparent reason
- Intermittent loss of mouse or keyboard
- Configuration files changed without user or system administrator action in operating system
- Configuration changes to software made without user or system administrator action
- BCS unresponsive
- When an asset is communicating outside the bounds of the data flow baseline
- HMI, OPC, and controllers not synchronized

- Unexpected changes to instructions, function calls, commands, or alarm thresholds being sent from HMI or OPC to controllers

- HMI or OPC not updating after operator made changes to instructions, commands, or alarm thresholds

- Expected changes to controllers are not appearing on controllers

- An irregular vendor patch coming from an external source, or unexpected source, to a device within the BCS

- A device on the BCS is communicating with an undocumented, unauthorized, or unknown IP address

- A device other than authorized devices is sending field controller traffic to a BCS device

- Traffic coming or going to an unknown device

- A BCS field controller is communicating with an unknown device

- A BCS device has expanded its communications to other devices within the BCS

As you can see, there are many "observables" in the real world and the virtual world that tell us that something is going on that we need to explore. Most alerts are not malicious but are due to authorized events or can otherwise be explained. The following are questions to ask:

- Was maintenance performed on the system or a software update installed recently?

- Did the equipment simply malfunction?

- Did the equipment lose network connectivity (outside the building)?

- Was a new BCS device installed?

- Was a BCS device reconfigured? Was it reconfigured correctly?

- Are there other authorized events that could be causing excessive network traffic?

- Was an old process removed from the BCS?

- Is the problem due to user error?

If an event is detected *and* it cannot be explained, then we are compelled to perform integrity checks on *every* server, workstation, router, network switch, firewall, and controller, and all printers and peripherals.

When an event that may be a cyber-physical attack is detected, an *event ticket* is created and the appropriate Incident Response Team is called upon to investigate.

EVENT DIAGNOSTICS TABLE

Check	Anomalous Behavior Observables
☐	Unusually heavy BCS network traffic
☐	No disk space or significantly reduced free disk space
☐	Unusually high CPU usage
☐	Creation of new user accounts
☐	Attempted or actual use of administrator-level accounts
☐	Locked-out accounts
☐	Accounts in use when the user is not at work
☐	Cleared log files
☐	Full log files with an unusually large number of events
☐	Antivirus or IDS alerts
☐	Disabled antivirus software and other security controls
☐	Unexpected patch changes
☐	Machines or intelligent field devices connecting to outside IP addresses
☐	Requests for information about the system (social engineering attempts)
☐	Unexpected changes in configuration settings
☐	Unexpected system shutdown
☐	Stoppage or displayed error messages on a web, database, or application server
☐	Unusually slow access to hosts on the network

(*continued*)

☐	Filenames containing unusual characters or new or unexpected files and directories
☐	Auditing configuration changes logged on the host records, disabling auditing function
☐	A large number of bounced emails with suspicious content
☐	Unusual deviation from typical network traffic flows
☐	Erratic building equipment behavior, more than one device exhibits the same behavior
☐	Any apparent override of safety, backup, or failover systems
☐	Equipment, servers, or network traffic that has bursts of temporary high usage when the operational process itself is steady and predictable
☐	Unknown or unusual traffic from corporate or other network external to BCS
☐	Unknown or unexpected firmware pulls or pushes
☐	Loss of building utilities (electricity, water, gas, sewer equipment failure)
Check	**Anomalous Behavior Observables**
☐	Very large number of complaints from building tenants
☐	Failure of multiple types of building equipment simultaneously
☐	Very high energy usage
☐	Obviously erroneous readings in BCS displays
☐	Discovery that system safety devices have been disabled
☐	Equipment running during the wrong season of the year

MASTER LIST OF DEFICIENCIES

Equipment	Deficiency

DECISION TIME

Decision Point	Actions				Category
1. Cyber "event" is discovered by IDS or unexpected equipment failure	2. Event is confirmed to be "Incident"	3. Recovery Procedures activated	4. Alarm sounds	5. Building evacuated	Initiation
	2. If no, then	3. Recovery Procedures is not activated	4. Return to normal operations	5. Evaluate response	Determination
6. Determine scope of incident and assess damage after building access is allowed	7. If small scope with no to minimal damage, then	8. Repair and begin clean up	9. Return to normal operations	10. Notify management and tenants of situation	Short Evacuation May Be Required
	7. Moderate to large scope or moderate to severe damage, then	8. Activate alternate site	9. Activate Incident Recovery Team	10. Notify management and tenants of situation	Moderate to Severe Damage to Building or Infrastructure
11. Assess damage	12. If damage is moderate and will be able to return in 30 days or less	13. Complete repairs as necessary while operating at alternate site	14. Return to building	15. Return to normal operations	Moderate Severe Damage to Building or Infrastructure
	12. If more than 30 days expected for repairs, locate to new building	13. Order supplies and equipment	14. Set up and operate at new facility while completing repairs	15. Return to normal operations	Severe Damage to Building or Infrastructure
	12. If total loss, locate to new facility	13. Rebuild	14. Set up at new facility while completing repairs	15. Return to normal operations	

PHASE 2: MITIGATION

Mitigation and Segmentation

- The Incident Response Team's first priority is to isolate any compromised devices and protect the building and personnel through segmentation. The segmentation must be based on a predetermined strategy taking into account specific equipment and building mission realities. After this step is complete, the Incident Response Teams ensure that local control has been achieved.

- The Facilities Incident Response Team conducts a preliminary Rapid Inspection of incident impact, known injuries, extent of damage, and disruption to building services and operations.

- The Incident Response Team informs the Recovery Procedures Coordinator who determines if or when access to the facility will be allowed.

- The Recovery Procedures Coordinator establishes and organizes a management control center and headquarters for the recovery operations.

- The Recovery Procedures Coordinator implements procedures necessary to mobilize operations, support and department relocation as well as employee and external individuals and organizations notification before, during, and after relocation.

- The Recovery Procedures Coordinator notifies and appraises management of the situation.

Building Equipment Damage Assessments

The Facilities Incident Recovery Team starts their damage assessment with a Rapid Inspection of all building equipment and systems and uses checklists to make sure they cover every possible anomaly. The FAC Team jots down the equipments' dial readings to compare with the BCS display readings. They check the equipment for out of range setpoints and ensure that equipment is working properly.

It is important to note that merely looking at the BCS display is a waste of time as those readings are probably false. A hacker will have a hard time spoofing a mechanical pressure gauge on a steam line or fuel train. The FAC Team looks for low water levels, low fuel levels, leaks, squeaks, squeals, vibration and odd smells (such as overheating or burning oil). They check fan belts, motors, pumps, and fans to make sure that they are operating. They confirm that things like the basin heater in the cooling tower are not on during summer months. Basically, they are physically looking for things that are odd or unexpected.

If they suspect a cyber-physical attack is underway and it appears as if the equipment is in the process of damaging itself, the FAC Team will immediately shut that piece of equipment down manually and ensure the equipment cannot be turned back on by the BCS. The FAC Team will lock out the equipment until the BCS has been examined carefully by the Tech Team.

The FAC Team prepares a list of salvageable equipment and makes a preliminary assessment listing equipment that can be repaired, equipment that cannot be repaired, and equipment that does not require repair. Once they know the equipment that was targeted, the FAC Team begins to assemble the manuals, drawings, parts lists, and equipment documentation so they can begin the repair or replacement process.

At this point, the FAC Team reports to the Recovery Procedures Coordinator with a preliminary estimate of the damage found and an educated estimate of the amount of time needed to effect repairs. Repairs that can be done in a matter of days are separated from those that will take months. The FAC Team also prepares a preliminary cost estimate for approval prior to commencing with requisition of replacement units.

One valuable tool that may be overlooked by management is the fact that although equipment has been damaged, sometimes a workaround can be pressed into service to partially restore service to allow continued occupation of the facility. For example, if the hot-water boiler was damaged beyond repair in the summertime, hot-water heating may not necessarily be a priority. Granted the HVAC system is designed to use reheat coils to optimize the temperature to a given space. Without hot-water heating, the maintenance crew can temper the conditioning by raising the temperature of the chilled water circulating throughout the building. Instead of cooling the water to 48 degrees, simply circulate 56-degree water throughout. Some spaces will be a little warmer than usual, but the majority of the building will be comfortable.

Of course, it would be difficult to operate the building without potable water, but tanker trucks can deliver potable water as a temporary measure. And, in a crisis, the ideal is to have working toilets in the building but at a time of war, porta-johns may be all you can get.

The important thing is to start thinking about workarounds because you will need them. Add workarounds to the planning process and start and plan to use them. If there is no convenient outside connection to hook up a potable water truck or a portable water tank, perhaps now would be a good time to install one (in a secure location).

BCS Network Integrity Checks

The TECH Team begins by reviewing processes to identify malicious activity and anomalous symptoms (not attributed to hardware or software malfunctions). The TECH Team performs integrity checks using the procedures developed specifically for your building to identify malicious cyber activity. The TECH Team reviews host log files looking for unauthorized user account activity or user account changes. They verify network communications compared to the baseline and check the Registry on all servers and workstations looking for changes or anomalies. If a server or workstation is unresponsive, the TECH Team boots the machine from a Rescue CD and uses tools to identify any problems. The TECH Team checks the routers, switch and firewalls to determine if running configuration, start-up configuration, or operating system files have been modified and they check the devices for a rootkit.

The TECH Team verifies the network data flow compared to the baseline. They review the firewall log file looking for anomalies. They check the IDS configuration files, rules, operating system, firmware, and log files to see if they have been modified. They also determine if the communications coming from the originating IP address should be communicating with the destination machines.

The TECH Team identifies the communications path between devices they are investigating and NetFlows. They will observe the data flow for anomalous traffic including ports, protocols, and services not included in the Baseline Data Flow Table. They will document the originating asset and destination asset's IP address.

Server/Workstation Process Checks

The TECH Team will check servers and workstation log file looking for unauthorized activity. They check for processes that do not appear to be legitimate. This includes processes that have no icon or name, are unsigned Microsoft images, reside in the Windows directory, include unfamiliar URLs, communicate with unknown IP address, or host suspicious DLL or services hiding as a DLL instead of a process.

The log review looks for unusual user activity, unfamiliar file names, unusually full log files or total cleared log files, unexpected configuration changes, unexpected system halts and reboots, file names with unusual characters and unexpected remote communications. The TECH Team captures the machine's network status and stores it to a file. They then compare the network communications with the expected communications for that machine.

If the machine is unresponsive, the team does a "hard" reboot on the machine with the Rescue CD in the drive. They then perform diagnostics on the machine to determine if there is a good Master Boot Record, is there a problem with the memory, is there a hardware error and do the files appear accessible?

BCS INTEGRITY CHECKS

Check	Device Integrity	Description
☐	Computer Unresponsive	**BOOT** from Rescue CD, use tools to uncover problems.
☐	Software Processes	**REVIEW** processes to identify malicious activity. Includes data base servers, control servers, HMIs, OPCs, master terminal units (MTUs), and engineering workstations.
☐	Log Files	**REVIEW** database servers, HMIs, control server, engineering workstations, OPCs, MTUs, and firewall log files for anomalies.
☐	Registry	**IDENTIFY** changes and anomalies in the registry.
☐	Rootkit	**CHECK** devices for a rootkit.
☐	Network Communications	**VERIFY** network communications to the expected communications based on baseline. **VERIFY** data flow, and compare to baseline.
☐	Unauthorized User Activity	**REVIEW** host log files for user account changes.
☐	Firewalls	**DETERMINE** if configuration files, access control lists, operating system have been modified. **REVIEW** log file for anomalies or if log files have been modified.
☐	Switches and Routers	**DETERMINE** if start-up configuration, running configuration, or operating system files have been modified.
☐	Controllers	**VERIFY** the operating system, configuration files, and firmware against baseline. Includes PLCs, intelligent electronic devices, and remote terminal units.
☐	Intrusion Detection System IDS Alerts – Inbound ICS Protocol	**DETERMINE** if IDS configuration files, rules, operating system, firmware, or log files have been modified. **DETERMINE** if the communications coming from the originating IP address should be communicating with the destination device.
☐	Peripherals and Other Network Devices	**DETERMINE** whether the device has configuration files or operating systems, and whether they have been modified.

BUILDING CONTROLS SYSTEM INFORMATION

Date Updated

Unique Application ID

Application Name

Owner (e.g., department, etc.)

Custodian (e.g., departmental IT staff, vendor)

Description

User Base/Scope

Business Function

Data Classification

Criticality

Date of Last Business Impact Analysis (BIA)

Operating System

Asset Tag

Serial Number

Licensing Information

Vendor (or, internally developed)

Maintenance Contract Expires

Maintenance Contact

Current Instances (e.g., production and test, test only, production only)

Program Language(s)

Internet Accessible

Requires own server

Desktop Data Storage (e.g., the files/configuration that are required if app allows or requires storage of data on workstations)

External File Requirements

Domain Information

Service Account(s)

Storage Requirements

Seats/Units

Load Balancing

License Requirements

Protocol Requirements

Port Requirements

Network Requirements

IP Address/Range

Minimum Client Requirements

Encryption Requirements

Third Party Requirements (e.g., applications or software required)

Code Libraries

Known Bottlenecks

Batch Processing Details (e.g., scheduled tasks, duration, subtasks, etc.)

Backup Software

Backup Type

Backup Frequency/Schedule

Media

Offsite Storage Location

Generations Offsite

Source Code Backed Up?

Additional Details

Maintenance Window Details

Vendor /Internal contact information

Recovery Point Objective (RPO)

Recovery Time Objective (RTO)

Priority

Additional Details

Supporting Documentation Location

Additional Details

Application is dependent on the following hardware resources:

Other processes dependent on this application:

Applications/services dependent on this resource:

Applications/services this resource is dependent on:

■ **Note**   This list should be completed and kept current.

BCS SERVER DETAILS

Date Updated

Unique Hardware ID

Hardware Name

Rack location

Custodian (e.g., department IT staff, vendor)

User Base/Scope

Description

Hardware Make/Model (e.g., Dell PowerEdge R200)

Hardware Type

Data Classification

Criticality

Recovery Time Objective (RTO)

Date of Last Business Impact Analysis (BIA)

Location (e.g., building & room)

Rack ID (if applicable)

Asset Tag

Serial Number

Model Number

Vendor

Warranty Expires

Maintenance Contact

BTU (cooling requirements)

KVA (power consumption rate)

Processor (# and type)

■ **Note**   This list should be completed and kept current.

BUILDING INSPECTION

Who does the inspection?	Facilities engineers, architects, structural, mechanical and electrical engineers, security officer, safety officer, and city or county building, health and fire inspectors.
What do they inspect?	General property inspection and collection of records and if necessary, information needed to repair or replace damaged equipment. A rapid inspection is followed by a detailed engineering inspection. Engineers will inspect building columns, walls, ceilings, roof, masonry, windows, and doors for obvious hazards. They will also inspect stairs and elevators for safety hazards. Stuck doors and sagging ceilings can be indicators of structural weakness.
Why are they doing the inspection?	To identify damage in the building and reduce or permanently eliminate future risk to lives and property. Inspectors will take photographs and document the damage for reporting purposes and planning building repairs.
When do they do the inspection?	Inspections are conducted immediately after the incident as soon as building is accessible and/or when allowed entry by local officials.
What is the result of the inspection?	Obtain the local permits, certificates of occupancy, and any other required documentation to demonstrate compliance with local building/zoning/life safety regulations.
What if the building does not pass inspection?	Develop a project plan and obtain necessary funding and approvals for building restoration and repairs. If the building is a complete loss, develop a plan to replace the building.

Agency	Contact Information
City Building Department	
Dept. of Public Works	
Fire Department	
Emergency Management	
CERT	
FEMA	
Electric Utility Company	
Natural Gas Utility Company	
Water and Sewer Utility	

EQUIPMENT OR SERVICE FAILURE REPORT

Building:		Date:		Report No.:	
Area affected and phenomenon or condition failure:		Partial Failure ☐		Complete Failure ☒	
Mode of Discovery:	Alarm ☐	Rounds/ Inspection ☐	Abnormal Equip Operation ☐	Occupant Complaint ☐	Preventive Maintenance ☐
Description of equipment or services that failed:					
Emergency or temporary measures and containment actions:					
Final or subsequent repairs:					
Repaired by:					
Defect:	Open ☐		Closed ☐		
Remedial Action Required:					
	Yes ☐ No ☐				
Describe:					
Maintenance personnel on duty at time of incident:					
Findings and Conclusions:					
Was this a cyber-attack?					
Explain:					

DAMAGE ASSESSMENT ACTIVITIES

Building:	Location:	Date:

Utilizing the following checklist as a guideline and survey the building and systems to assess damage.

Building	NOTES:
Exterior	
Interior	
Walls	
Ceiling	
Floor	
Controls	
Electrical	
UPS	
Transformers	
Emergency/Building	
HVAC	
Air Handling	
Air Conditioning	
Fire Suppression	
Building Operations Center	
Servers	
External Disk Drives	
Tape Backup	
Network Cabling	
Communications	
Workstations	
Other Equipment	
Tape Media	
Spare Parts	
Documentation	

Participants:	
Is the area safe for employees or vendors to work in?	
Can equipment under examination function, and if so, at what percent of normal capacity?	
What must be done to recover damaged equipment?	
How long will it take to repair or replace the damaged equipment?	

Using the damage assessment, determine the estimated time to recover based on the following guidelines.

- **Level I: Minimal damage** to facility and/or equipment. Estimated time to complete repairs is less than 4 hours.

- **Level II: Moderate damage** to facility and/or equipment. Estimated time to complete repairs is between 4 hours and 2 business days.

- **Level III: Extensive damage** to facility and/or equipment. Estimated time to complete repairs is greater than 2 business days.

☐	Identify equipment or spare parts that are immediately salvageable or in need of repair.
☐	Verbally notify the Management Team of survey, assessment of damage, and estimated time to recover.
☐	Document findings from the survey and damage assessment.
☐	Attend the recovery briefing to apprise Incident Recovery Team members of findings.
☐	A log is prepared and maintained to record all salvageable equipment and its disposition and location.

RAPID INSPECTION CHECKLISTS

Use the checklists on the following pages to document the condition of building equipment after a rapid inspection and describe the extent of damage found on the following table.

COOLING TOWER
Rapid Inspection Checklist

Cooling Tower No.: CT-1

Check	Physical Inspection
☐	Two-way makeup water
☐	Two-way blowdown to drain
☐	Two-way CWR and CWS isolation valve
☐	Cooling tower fan VFD
☐	Two-way bypass valve on CWR condenser
☐	Vibration cutout switch
☐	Pressure ports and flow sensors
☐	Temperature sensing wells
	Electrical
☐	Tower fan drive
☐	Motor fan rotation
☐	System interlocks functional
☐	Power available to tower disconnect
☐	Power available to electric sump heater
	Controls
☐	Makeup control valve shut off

1. Activate cooling tower fan start using control system command. This should first start the condenser water pump, establish flow, delay fan start to equalize flow in distribution basis and sump.

2. After chiller start-up, control system should modulate bypass valve and two-speed fan motor to maintain condenser water setpoint. Verify function of bypass valve under varying loads.

3. Verify cooling tower interlock with chiller.

4. Verify that the makeup water float valve is functioning.

5. Activate chemical treatment feed valve, verify makeup of chemical treatment system, pump and controls.

6. Stop all building cooling equipment so that cooling tower pumps stop. Observe tower for at least 15 minutes and verify no overflow occurs.

7. Start cooling tower pumps in hand mode and observe pumps for air binding/cavitation.

■ **Note**   Modify for your specific building.

BOILER OR PRESSURE VESSEL
Rapid Inspection Checklist

Boiler No.: BR-1

Check	Physical Inspection
☐	Check that access doors are operable and sealed.
☐	Verify the boiler water level.
☐	Check that all stack dampers are open.
☐	Examine the boiler furnace for foreign material.
☐	Check the furnace and flue passes for fuel accumulation.
☐	Make sure that the manual fuel valves are open.
☐	Check all ventilation and combustion air openings and louvers are clean and free of debris.
☐	Verify operation of all operating and limit controls, interlocks and gauge
☐	Monitor main flame.
	Boiler Fuel
☐	Fuel is available to boiler.
☐	Check fuel pressure.
☐	Check fuel throughput.
	Electrical
☐	Check that power is available to unit disconnect.
☐	Check that power is available to unit control panel.
☐	Check flame signal.
☐	Check automatic safety shutoff.
☐	Check trip circuit for proper operation.

(*continued*)

Check	Physical Inspection
	Coils
☐	Check supply water temperature.
☐	Check flue gas temperature.
	Controls
☐	Control valves operable.
☐	Control actuators operable.
☐	Dampers operable.
☐	Damper actuators operable.
☐	Check 02 valve.
☐	Check gas fuel volume.
☐	Air Measuring Stations operational.
☐	Check feed water pump operation.
	Testing, Adjusting, and Balancing (TAB)
☐	Filters are not clogged or blocked.
☐	Boiler fully operational.

BOILER VISUAL INSPECTION

Cyber-Attack Tree

Ways that an Adversary Can Attack Boilers
☐   Power failure: The entire system is de-energized, closing all automatic valves and halting all boiler operations.
☐   Low-water switch opens. BCS thinks there is insufficient water in the boiler.
☐   External gas-supply shut-off valve is closed, so BCS thinks a low gas condition results.
☐   High gas pressure switch opens. BCS thinks burner operation is interrupted and the boiler locks out.
☐   BCS thinks boiler water has exceeded both the operating and high-limit temperature the high limit switch opens, and the boiler will remain locked out until the water high limit switch is manually reset.
☐   **FLAME ERROR** BCS thinks there is a flame failure, the main fuel valves are de-energized, and a manual reset lockout occurs.
☐   **BLOCKED FLUE** error code sent indicating the high exhaust backpressure switch has tripped.
☐   **AIR SWITCH NOT OPEN** or **AIR SWITCH NOT CLOSED** error codes so BCS thinks there is improper airflow through the boiler.

Begin by looking for evidence of bulges, cracks, or other deformities. Check for cracked glass on gauges and bent pointers on meters. Check draft, manifold pressure, and combustion. Observe condition of flame. Flame should not impinge on furnace walls. Test the low-water fuel cutoffs for proper sequencing and operation. Blow down the boiler. Check water column or glass gauge. Observe operation of condensate or vacuum pumps. Check operation of chemical feed pots and feed pumps. Test flame detection devices and associated automatic fuel cutoff valves. Inspect condensate return valves radiators and traps. Blow down strainers. Inspect fuel supply systems and piping in boilers. Replace cartridges for in-line oil filters. Check safety valves and test with tri-level.

Inspect burner assembly. Clean, check and adjust electrodes. If the boiler is equipped with an air-to-fuel ratio control system, ensure the control system is operating in accordance with the manufacturers specifications. Inspect control equipment for proper sequencing and operation.

Check expansion tank and air eliminator equipment. Check breaching and stack for tightness.

BOILER OR PRESSURE VESSEL

Boiler No.: BR-1

HOT WATER SYSTEM CHECKLIST					
Building:		**Location:**		**Job Number:**	
Equipment:		**Hot Water Loop:**			
Test Equipment:			Tested By:		
Boiler Name:		Boiler Function:		Boiler Type:	Capacity:
Boiler Manufacturer:		Model No.		Serial No.	MAWP:

VISUAL AND MECHANICAL INSPECTION

Internal Inspection	SAT	UNSAT	Operational	SAT	UNSAT
Combustion Chamber	☐	☐	**Gas Boilers**		
Brickwork	☐	☐	Start in low Fire	☐	☐
Insulation	☐	☐	Loss of Combustion Air	☐	☐
Elec/Mech Interlocks	☐	☐	Low Gas Pressure	☐	☐
Fire/Water Tubes	☐	☐	High Gas Pressure	☐	☐
Burner Nozzle	☐	☐	**Fuel Oil Burners**		
Steam Drum	☐	☐	Start in Low Fire	☐	☐
Stack/Flue	☐	☐	Loss of Combustion Air	☐	☐
Blow off Valve	☐	☐	Loss of Atomizing Air	☐	☐
External Inspection			Low Oil Pressure	☐	☐
Programmer	☐	☐	Burner Straw Switch (if applicable)	☐	☐
Low Water/Fuel Cutouts	☐	☐	Proximity Switch (if applicable)	☐	☐
Water Column	☐	☐	**All Boilers**		
Pressure Gauge	☐	☐	Flame Sensor	☐	☐

(continued)

HOT WATER SYSTEM CHECKLIST					
Review Record Logs (weekly/month)	☐	☐	Low Water Cut Off (left/right)	☐	☐
Condensing Neutralizer Installed	☐	☐	Feed Pump/ Recirculating Pump	☐	☐
			Normal Trip	☐	☐
Hydrostatic Test	☐	☐	Flame Pattern Inspection	☐	☐
Backflow Preventer	☐	☐	Water Treatment	☐	☐
			High Trip	☐	☐
Date of last Combustion Tuning			Emergency Stop	☐	☐
Date of last waterside inspection			Combustion Tuning	☐	☐
Date of last 150% Strength Hydro			Combustion (Air/Fuel) Control System	☐	☐
			Test Relief Valve Under Pressure	☐	☐

Boiler Efficiency						
	Oxygen %	CO ppm	CO2%	SO2 ppm	NO ppm	Stack Temp.
Gas Fired						
Oil Fired						

Burner Assy.	Model	BTU Range	S/N	Programmer

	Manufacturer	Size	PSI	BTU/Hr
Safety/Relief Valve				
Gauge				
Inspector:				
		Certification Expires:		

■ **Note**   Fill out one form for each boiler. Modify for your specific building.

CHILLED WATER SYSTEM

Rapid Inspection Checklist

Chiller No.: CH-1

Check	Physical Inspection
☐	Check that access doors are operable and sealed.
☐	Verify refrigerant level.
☐	Check chilled-water pump, flow and control valve.
☐	Check for closed shutoff valves.
☐	Check sensors, controllers, and setpoint, actuator/positioners.
☐	Check filters and fans.
☐	Check controls, switches, starters, and disconnects.
☐	Check expansion tank and air separator.
☐	Check safeties and interlocks to fire protection system.
☐	Inspect for oil leaks and check oil level.
☐	Check pH of chilled water.
☐	Check pH of condenser water.
☐	Inspect purge unit operation.
☐	Sample condenser water.
☐	Inspect V-belts (vapor compression chillers).
☐	Sample lithium bromide for testing (absorption chillers only).
	Electrical
☐	Power is available to unit disconnect.
☐	Power is available to unit control panel.
☐	Check refrigerant heaters.
☐	Check power supply.
	Controls
☐	Control valves operable.
☐	Control actuators operable.
☐	Check Program Logic Controller.
☐	Damper actuators operable.
	Testing, Adjusting, and Balancing (TAB)
☐	Filters are not clogged or blocked.
☐	Chillers fully operational.

CHILLER VISUAL INSPECTION

Cyber-Attack Tree

Ways that an Adversary Can Attack Chillers
☐   Low-pressure trip: BCS thinks that refrigerant is low; has low or no water flow; or that there is a clogged water filter or screen.
☐   High-pressure trip: BCS thinks that water-cooled condenser has poor or no flow; air-cooled condenser is blocked with debris or has a fan that is not working; or that the chilled water tank temperature is too high.
☐   Oil failure trip: BCS thinks that either low superheat or low oil.
☐   Freezestat: BCS thinks poor water flow or that the thermostat is set too low.
☐   Blown fuses or starter trips: BCS over-amped motor, compressor, or wires.
☐   System not reaching thermostat setpoint. BCS thinks that evaporator is iced up.
☐   Proof of flow: BCS thinks either flow or pressure switches in water circuit are suffering from low or no flow, water filter is blocked, or water valve is shut off.

1. Begin by looking for indicators or codes that come up on the diagnostic readouts.

2. Make a visual inspection of the electrical panel, water piping, and pump tank system.

3. Look for obvious problems, such as burned or broken wires, water pump not running, water valves shut off, and improper system water temperature.

4. Is the chiller running and not cooling, or not running at all?

5. Is the pump circulating water? What is the water temperature?

6. If the chiller isn't running, check the high-voltage circuits.

7. Does the chiller have power? Check all the fuses.

8. Start at the power side of the control transformer and check wire by wire. Trace the power wire from safety to safety.

9. Check the water flow switch and the freezestat control.

10. Strap temperature probes on the suction, discharge, and liquid lines.

11. Watch all the pressures, temperatures, and amperages.

CHILLED WATER SYSTEM CHECKLIST

Chiller No.: CH-1

Building:		Location:		Job Number:	
Equipment:		Cooling Water Loop:			
Test Equipment:		Tested By:			
Chiller Manufacturer:		Model No.	Serial No.		BTU Rating:
Pump Manufacturer:		Model No.	Serial No.		Rated Flow:
HP @ RPM		Rated NPSH		Rated Pressure	

VISUAL AND MECHANICAL INSPECTION

	CONDITION		CONDITION
Exterior of Equipment		Equipment Identification	
Completeness of Assembly		Bracing	
Equipment Rotation		Labeling and Tagging	
Elec/Mech Interlocks		Safety Interlocks	
Instruments		Working Space	
Proper Grounding		Anchorage	
Proper Insulation		System Flushed and Cleaned	
Tightness of Bolts		Compare to Drawings	
Proper Lubrication		Control System	
Refrigerant Installed		Water Treatment Installed	

CONDITION: A-ACCEPTABLE; R-NEEDS REPAIR, REPLACEMENT, OR ADJUSTMENT;
C- CORRECTED; NA-NOT APPLICABLE

CALIBRATION AND SETPOINT					
	DESCRIPTION		NOTES		
Sensors	Pressure, temperature, and condition sensors checked OK				
Controllers	Control system interfaces with BCS				
Actuators	Exercise annually for valve control				
Relief Valves Checked	Exercise annually for valve operation limits				
HYDRONIC SYSTEM TESTS					
	Operating Mode	Temperature	Pressure	Flows	Levels
Chiller					
Pump					
Hydrostatic Test					
Balance Test					
Cooling Coil Number					
Expansion Tank/Air Separator					
Control Valves					
System test	Performed Annually				
Notes:					

AIR HANDLING UNIT CHECKLIST

Rapid Inspection Checklist

AIR HANDLER No.: AHU - 1

Check	Physical Inspection
☐	Verify that access doors are operable and sealed.
☐	Verify that condensate drainage is unobstructed. (Verify drainage by pouring a cup of water into drain pan.)
☐	Check fan belt operation and adjustment.
	Electrical
☐	Power is available to unit disconnect.
☐	Power is available to unit control panel.
☐	Proper motor rotation verified.
☐	Power is stable at proper voltage.
☐	UV light is fully operational.
	Coils
☐	Chilled-water piping properly connected.
☐	Hot-water piping properly connected.
	Controls
☐	Control valves operable.
☐	Control actuators operable.
☐	Dampers operable.
☐	Damper actuators operable.
☐	Verify proper operation of duct static pressure sensor.
☐	Fan air volume controller operable.
☐	Air Measuring Stations operational.
☐	Air handler controls system operational.
	Testing, Adjusting, and Balancing (TAB)
☐	Filters are not clogged or blocked.

■ **Note**   Fill out one form for each air handling unit. Modify for your specific building.

AIR HANDLING UNIT VISUAL INSPECTION

Cyber-Attack Tree

AIR HANDLER No.: AHU-1

1. Begin by looking for indicators or codes that come up on the diagnostic readouts.

2. Is the system low in airflow?

3. Check parameters such as pressure, power, speed, elevation, and temperature.

4. Check actual airflow compared to the desired airflow.

5. Document test measurements and their locations.

6. Check all driveline components, such as bearings, couplings, V-belts, and motors.

7. Ensure that the fan wheel is properly aligned with the inlet bell and housing, is free to turn, and turns in the right direction.

8. Check the fan and system for any obstructions, build-up, leaks, or missing parts.

9. Run the fan at full speed, verifying that it's running close to the design speed.

10. Check that the fan is running smoothly and that the bearings aren't running hot.

11. Make sure that the fan isn't overloading the motor.

Air handlers are controlled by the BCS, which has the ability to turn the system's fans on or off, and open and close the dampers. Verify the BCS configuration setpoints and time clock to ensure that it's giving the fan the correct command to operate and that is opening and closing the appropriate dampers.

Air handlers have variable frequency drives that adjust the fan speeds based on static pressure in the ductwork. When a VFD isn't receiving a signal from the BCS, it defaults to either its minimum speed or to its high speed.

COMPUTER ROOM AIR CONDITIONER
Rapid Inspection Checklist

CRAC No.: CR-1

Check	Physical Inspection
☐	Verify that access doors are operable and sealed.
☐	Verify that condensate drainage is unobstructed. (Verify drainage by pouring a cup of water into drain pan.)
☐	Check fan belt operation and adjustment.
	Electrical
☐	Power is available to unit disconnect.
☐	Proper motor rotation verified.
☐	Proper motor rotation verified.
☐	Power is stable at proper voltage.
	Coils/Humidifier
☐	Chilled-water piping properly connected.
☐	Hot-water piping properly connected.
	Controls
☐	Control valves operable.
☐	Unit control system operable and verified.
☐	Verify proper operation of thermostat.
	Testing, Adjusting, and Balancing (TAB)
☐	CRAC unit is operating properly.

PUMP: PRIMARY CHILLED WATER

Rapid Inspection Checklist

Pump No.: PCHW-1

Check	Physical Inspection
☐	Piping system inspected.
	Electrical
☐	Power is available to pump disconnect.
☐	Pump rotation verified.
☐	Control system interlocks functional.
☐	VFD operation verified (where applicable).
	Testing, Adjusting, and Balancing (TAB)
☐	Pressure/temperature gauges operating.

Pump Control Questions

1. What causes the pump to initially start?
2. What causes the pump to cycle?
3. How is capacity controlled?
4. What is the differential pressure control point?
5. Is there is a lead/lag strategy?
6. Are pumps staged?

PUMP: SECONDARY CHILLED WATER

Rapid Inspection Checklist

Pump No.: SCHW-1

Check	Physical Inspection
☐	Piping system inspected.
	Electrical
☐	Power is available to pump disconnect.
☐	Pump rotation verified.
☐	Control system interlocks functional.
☐	VFD operation verified (where applicable).
	Testing, Adjusting, and Balancing (TAB)
☐	Pressure/temperature gauges operating.

Pump Control Questions

1. What causes the pump to initially start?
2. What causes the pump to cycle?
3. How is capacity controlled?
4. What is the differential pressure control point?
5. Is there is a lead/lag strategy?
6. Are pumps staged?

PUMP: PRIMARY DOMESTIC HOT WATER

Rapid Inspection Checklist

Pump No.: PDHW-1

Check	Physical Inspection
☐	Piping system inspected.
	Electrical
☐	Power is available to pump disconnect.
☐	Pump rotation verified.
☐	Control system interlocks functional.
☐	VFD operation verified (where applicable).
	Testing, Adjusting, and Balancing (TAB)
☐	Pressure/temperature gauges operating.

Pump Control Questions

1. What causes the pump to initially start?
2. What causes the pump to cycle?
3. How is capacity controlled?
4. What is the differential pressure control point?
5. Is there is a lead/lag strategy?
6. Are pumps staged?

PUMP: SECONDARY DOMESTIC HOT WATER

Rapid Inspection Checklist

Pump No.: SDHW-1

Check	Physical Inspection
☐	Piping system inspected.
	Electrical
☐	Power is available to pump disconnect.
☐	Pump rotation verified.
☐	Control system interlocks functional.
☐	VFD operation verified (where applicable).
	Testing, Adjusting, and Balancing (TAB)
☐	Pressure/temperature gauges operating.

Pump Control Questions

1. What causes the pump to initially start?
2. What causes the pump to cycle?
3. How is capacity controlled?
4. What is the differential pressure control point?
5. Is there is a lead/lag strategy?
6. Are pumps staged?

FAN COIL UNIT
Rapid Inspection Checklist

Fan Coil Unit No.: FCU-1

Check	Physical Inspection
☐	Verify that access doors are operable and sealed.
☐	Verify that condensate drainage is unobstructed.
☐	Check fan belt operation and adjustment.
	Electrical
☐	Power is available to unit disconnect.
☐	Power is available to unit control panel.
☐	Proper motor rotation verified.
☐	Verify that power is stable at proper voltage.
	Coils
☐	Chilled-water piping properly connected.
☐	Hot-water piping properly connected.
	Controls
☐	Control valves operable.
☐	Control actuators operable.
☐	Verify proper operation of thermostat.
	Testing, Adjusting, and Balancing (TAB)
☐	Pressure/temperature gauges operating.

■ **Note** Fill out one form for each fan coil unit. Modify for your specific building.

DIESEL BACKUP GENERATOR
Rapid Inspection Checklist

Generator No.: DG-1

Check	Physical Inspection
☐	Access doors are operable and sealed.
☐	Recovery system ductwork is unobstructed and clean.
☐	Recovery system wheel is operational.
☐	Cooling system is operating properly.
	Electrical
☐	Power is available to unit disconnect.
☐	Power is available to unit control panel.
☐	Proper engine rotation verified.
☐	Power is stable at proper voltage.
	Generator Fuel
☐	Fuel is available to generator.
☐	Diesel fuel is not contaminated.
	Controls
☐	Engine control properly programmed.
☐	Control dampers/actuators operable.
☐	Outside Air Flow Measurement Arrays operable.
	Testing, Adjusting, and Balancing (TAB)
☐	Filters removed and replaced.

DIESEL SYSTEM CHECKLIST

Generator No.: DG-1

DIESEL SYSTEM CHECKLIST					
Building:		Location:		Job Number:	
Equipment:		System Designation:			
Test Equipment:		Tested By:			
Pump Manufacturer:		Model No.		Serial No.	Flow Rating gpm:
Type:		HP @ RPM		Pressure Rating psig:	
Heater Manufacturer:		Model No.		Serial No.	Flow Rating gpm:
Cooler Manufacturer:		Model No.		Serial No.	Flow Rating gpm:

VISUAL AND MECHANICAL INSPECTION					
		CONDITION			CONDITION
Exterior of Equipment			Equipment Identification		
Completeness of Assembly			Bracing		
Equipment Rotation			Labeling and Tagging		
Elec/Mech Interlocks			Safety Interlocks		
Instruments			Working Space		
Proper Grounding			Anchorage		
Proper Insulation			Leaks		
Tightness of Bolts			Compare to Drawings		
Proper Lubrication			Control System		

CONDITION: A-ACCEPTABLE; R-NEEDS REPAIR, REPLACEMENT, OR ADJUSTMENT;
C- CORRECTED; NA-NOT APPLICABLE

CALIBRATION AND SETPOINT		
	DESCRIPTION	**NOTES**
Sensors	Main tank levels are consistent with sensor readings	
Controllers	Main tank controllers indicate all conditions normal	
Actuators	NA	

HYDRONIC SYSTEM TESTS					
	Operating Mode	**Temperature**	**Pressure**	**Flows**	**Levels**
Pump					
Heater					
Cooler					
Engine					
Hydrostatic Test					
System test	**Performed Annually**				
Notes:					

LUBE OIL SYSTEM
Rapid Inspection Checklist

Lube Oil System No.: LO-1

Check	Physical Inspection
☐	Access doors are operable and sealed.
☐	Recovery system ductwork is unobstructed and clean.
☐	Recovery system wheel operational.
☐	Cooling system is operating properly.
	Electrical
☐	Power is available to unit disconnect.
☐	Power is available to unit control panel.
☐	Proper engine rotation verified.
☐	Power is stable at proper voltage.
	Lube Oil
☐	Lube oil is available.
☐	Lube oil is not contaminated.
	Controls
☐	Engine control properly programmed.
☐	Control dampers/actuators operable.
☐	Outside Air Flow Measurement Arrays operable.
	Testing, Adjusting, and Balancing (TAB)
☐	Filters removed and replaced.
☐	TAB report approved.

LUBE OIL SYSTEM CHECKLIST

Lube Oil System No.: LO-1

LUBE OIL SYSTEM CHECKLIST

Building:	**Location:**	**Job Number:**	
Equipment:	**System Designation:**		
Test Equipment:		**Tested By:**	

Pump Manufacturer:	Model No.	Serial No.	Flow Rating gpm
Type:	**HP @ RPM**	**Pressure Rating psig:**	
Heater Manufacturer:	**Model No.**	**Serial No.**	**Flow Rating gpm**
Cooler Manufacturer:	**Model No.**	**Serial No.**	**Flow Rating gpm**

VISUAL AND MECHANICAL INSPECTION

	CONDITION		CONDITION
Exterior of Equipment		Equipment Identification	
Completeness of Assembly		Bracing	
Equipment Rotation		Labeling and Tagging	
Elec/Mech Interlocks		Safety Interlocks	
Instruments		Working Space	
Proper Grounding		Anchorage	
Proper Insulation		Leaks	
Tightness of Bolts		Compare to Drawings	
Proper Lubrication		Control System	

CONDITION: A-ACCEPTABLE; R-NEEDS REPAIR, REPLACEMENT, OR ADJUSTMENT;
C- CORRECTED; NA-NOT APPLICABLE

CALIBRATION AND SETPOINT		
	DESCRIPTION	NOTES
Sensors	Main tank levels are consistent with sensor readings	
Controllers	Main tank controllers indicate all conditions normal	
Actuators	NA	

HYDRONIC SYSTEM TESTS					
	Operating Mode	Temperature	Pressure	Flows	Levels
Pump					
Heater					
Cooler					
Engine					
Hydrostatic Test					
System test	**Performed Annually**				

Notes:

VENTILATION SYSTEM CHECKLIST

Rapid Inspection Checklist

Ventilation System No.: V-1

Check	Physical Inspection
☐	Fan belt operating and adjusted.
	Electrical
☐	Power is available to fan disconnect.
☐	Proper motor rotation verified.
☐	Power is stable at proper voltage.
	Controls
☐	Control interlocks are properly operating.
☐	Control interlocks are operable.
☐	Dampers/actuators are properly operating.
☐	Dampers/actuators are operable.
☐	Thermostat is operating properly.
	Testing, Adjusting, and Balancing (TAB)
☐	Exhaust fan is operating properly.

■ **Note** Fill out one form for each ventilation system. Modify for your specific building.

VENTILATION SYSTEM
Rapid Inspection Checklist

Ventilation System No.: V-1

VENTILATION SYSTEM CHECKLIST						
Building:		Location:			Job Number:	
Equipment:				Air Loop Designation:		
Test Equipment:				Tested By:		
Fan Manufacturer:		Model No.			Serial No.	Rated Flow cfm:
Fan Type:		HP @ RPM			Rated Pressure psig:	

VISUAL AND MECHANICAL INSPECTION					
	CONDITION				CONDITION
Exterior of Equipment			Equipment Identification		
Completeness of Assembly			Bracing		
Equipment Rotation			Labeling and Tagging		
Elec/Mech Interlocks			Safety Interlocks		
Instruments			Working Space		
Proper Grounding			Anchorage		
Proper Insulation			Leaks		
Tightness of Bolts			Compare to Drawings		
Proper Lubrication			Control System		
Condensate Drip Pans			Filters		

CONDITION: A-ACCEPTABLE; R-NEEDS REPAIR, REPLACEMENT, OR ADJUSTMENT;
C- CORRECTED; NA-NOT APPLICABLE

HYDRONIC SYSTEM TESTS

	Operating Mode	Temperature	Pressure	Flows	Levels
Chiller					
Pump					
Hydrostatic Test					
Balance Test					
Cooling Coil Number					
Expansion Tank/Air Separator					
Control Valves					
System Test	Performed Annually				

Notes:

CALIBRATION AND SETPOINT

	DESCRIPTION	NOTES
Sensors	Checked sensors with standard	
Controllers	Cycled controllers for response	
Actuators	Checked full operation from fully open to fully closed	
Fire Dampers Checked	Actuated fire dampers. Checked for proper operation	
Smoke Dampers Checked	Actuated smoke dampers. Checked for proper operation	

■ **Note**   Fill out one form for each piece of ventilation equipment. Modify for your specific building.

ELECTRICAL SWITCHGEAR INSPECTION

Cyber-Attack Tree

Ways that an Adversary Can Attack an Electrical Switchgear
☐   Sends invalid disconnect messages to meters.
☐   Compromises head end.
☐   Blocks DR messages.
☐   Causes inappropriate DR messages through improper DRAS configuration.
☐   Adds spurious trip parameters to trip unit offline.
☐   Trips equipment offline through vendor remote connection.
☐   Allows direct access from another network through improper firewall rule configuration.
☐   Sends DR message that cause services to send "last gasp" or "self-test failed" messages direct to devices.
☐   Reconfigures meter via optical port.
☐   Floods communications channel with other messages, preventing legitimate DR messages from being received and transmitted.
☐   Modifies DRAS configuration to send DR messages at incorrect times or to incorrect devices.
☐   Manufactures an artificial cascade to trigger a blackout through sequential tripping of select feeders and components, causing automated tripping due to power and voltage fluctuations.
☐   Stops flow of wireless communications between devices.
☐   Overwhelms alarm-processing capability by sending unnecessary alarms.

ELECTRICAL SWITCHGEAR CHECKLIST

Rapid Inspection Checklist

Switchgear No.: 5 - 1

Check	Physical Inspection
☐	Check nameplate information.
☐	Inspect covers, panels, and doors.
☐	Check for smooth and proper movement of racking mechanisms, shutter, rollers, rails, and guides.
☐	Check alignment of primary and secondary contacts.
☐	Check operation of mechanical interlocks.
	Electrical
☐	Check phasing connection of busbar.
☐	Perform mechanical check and visual inspection for breaker.
☐	Perform electrical check and visual inspection for transformers.
☐	Perform mechanical check and visual inspection on disconnect switches.

▦ **Note** Fill out one form for each piece of equipment. Modify for your specific building.

REPAIR WORK ORDER LISTING

Priority	Task Number	Summary	Estimated Completion Date

RESTART OPERATING CONDITIONS

Reassessment

Repaired equipment shall be reassessed by comparing current conditions with normal operating conditions. A report shall be prepared with recommendations when building can be reoccupied.

Conditioned Space Temperature						
Operating Range:		to		deg F. Current Conditions:		deg F.

Unconditioned Space Temperature						
Operating Range:		to		deg F. Current Conditions:		deg F.

Duct Temperature						
Operating Range:		to		deg F. Current Conditions:		deg F.

Outside Air Temperature						
Operating Range:		to		deg F. Current Conditions:		deg F.

High Temperature Hot Water						
Operating Range:		to		deg F. Current Conditions:		deg F.

Chilled Water						
Operating Range:		to		deg F. Current Conditions:		deg F.

Heating Hot Water						
Operating Range:		to		deg F. Current Conditions:		deg F.

BUILDING CONTROLS POINT-TO-POINT CHECKS

HVAC										
Building:		Equipment:							Date:	
Point		Output				Input		Accept		Comment
Description	Name	DO	AI 0%	AI 50%	AI 100%	DI	AI	Y/N		

Checked By:	X_____	Date:
Verified By:	X_____	Date:

112

OTHER EQUIPMENT TO BE CHECKED

System	Description
Fire Detection System	
Parking Controls System	Has been done before. British airport garage was hacked, preventing parking controls from allowing autos to enter garage causing flight delays.
Traffic Barriers	
Elevators	
Fire Pump	
Smoke Evac System	
Lighting Controls	
Security Systems	
CCTV	
Access Control System	
Storm Drainage System	
Incinerators	
Fire Sprinkler System	
Domestic Hot Water System	
Cable TV System	
Public Address System	
Energy Recovery Systems	
Solar Energy System	
Medium-Voltage Electrical Distribution System	
Low-Voltage Electrical Distribution System	
Electric Power Monitoring System	
Duress Alarm Systems	
Sewerage Pump System	
Wastewater Pump System	
Storm Drainage Utilities	
Sanitary Sewerage Utilities	
Door Locking System	

PHASE 3: RECOVERY

Effective recovery after a cyber-physical attack requires ensuring that new reintegration devices will not be reinfected. The only way to avoid this problem is to verify that each device on the network is clean of any cyber incident remnants. All devices in the network should be replaced or reflashed with known, good firm/ software to provide confidence that reinfection will not occur.

Task No.	Prior Task	Description	IRT Team	Est. Start	Est. Finish
		RESTART undamaged equip—manual control	FAC		
		PURCHASE new building equipment	FAC		
		INSTALL new building equipment	FAC		
		RUN new equip—manual mode	FAC		
		RECEIVE new BCS IT equipment	Tech		
		INSTALL BCS software from vendor CD-ROMs	Tech		
		INSTALL new BCS servers	Tech		
		BOOT the BCS servers	Tech		
		TEST operating system	Tech		
		TEST network	Tech		
		TEST BCS	Tech		
		CONNECT building equipment to new BCS	MGMT/FAC/Tech		
		TEST BCS with building equipment	MGMT/FAC/Tech		
		ADVISE upper management	MGMT		
		REASSESS the situation	MGMT		
		SCHEDULE move dates for tenant return	MGMT/FAC/Tech		
		ESTABLISH new building operating schedule	MGMT/FAC/Tech		
		MOVE tenants back to building	MGMT		
		RESUME normal operations	MGMT/FAC/Tech		
		MONITOR help desk for tenant concerns	MGMT/FAC/Tech		
		PREPARE media statements	MGMT/SEC		
		PREPARE after-action report	MGMT/FAC/Tech		
		UPDATE Recovery Procedures w/ lessons learned	MGMT/FAC/Tech		

RECOVERY EVENT RECORDING FORM

1. Key events during the recovery phase must be recorded.

2. Separate form should be prepared for every major piece of equipment affected.

3. Event log shall be maintained by the Recovery Procedures Coordinator.

4. Event log should be started at the announcement of a cyber-physical attack and a copy of the log passed on to the Incident Recovery Teams once the initial dangers have been controlled.

5. The following event log should be completed to record all key events during the recovery phase.

Description of Cyber-Physical Attack:

Recovery Start Date:

Equipment and systems affected:

Recovery Start Date	Work Complete Date	Resources Involved	Person in Charge

BUILDING CONTROLS SYSTEM

The following Recovery and Reintegration checklists apply to all devices on the BCS network:
Servers
Workstations
Routers/Switches/Modems/Printers
Remote Terminal Units (RTU)/MTU/PLC
Intelligent Electronic Devices (IED)s; Controllers, Breakers, Switches, Re-closers, Regulators
Human-Machine Interface (HMI)
Firewalls
Media Converters (Serial to Fiber, Serial to Ethernet)

	BCS Recovery
☐	**DOCUMENT** steps taken during recovery procedures for forensic analysis of the cyber incident and possible use as evidence later on.
☐	**MAINTAIN** primary power (if possible) to the BCS device until an image of the onboard memory can be saved.
☐	**SAVE** an image of any hard drive(s) and volatile memory (if possible) for forensic analysis. This may require a reboot. **CAPTURE** volatile memory first, and then image the drive.
☐	**REMOVE and REPLACE** the affected BCS device.
☐	**DO NOT REIMAGE** any devices. Reimaging the affected device drive(s) will destroy forensic evidence of the cyber incident.
☐	**VERIFY** that the latest operating system, software, and firmware patches are installed on the device. **INSTALL** updates prior to reintegration in the BCS.
☐	**UPDATE** passwords on all BCS devices (including seldom-used obscure modules).
☐	**UPDATE** the antivirus software and intrusion detection software and **RUN** a full system scan.

	BCS Reintegration
☐	**DO NOT RECONNECT** the device to other devices in the network until each device in the affected network layer or affected sub-system has been recovered per these procedures.
☐	**VERIFY** that each device in the isolated layer or sub-system has been properly recovered. **CONSULT** the cyber incident records to confirm that *recovery* has been performed on these devices prior to reintegration on the BCS network.
☐	When each device in the layer or sub-system has been properly recovered and documented, **RECONNECT** all of the devices.
☐	**DO NOT RECONNECT** to the enterprise network.
☐	**VERIFY** that the forensics specialists have eliminated cyber-incident artifacts using detection tools (IDS, Log Review, NMap, Netstat, Wireshark, etc.) and documented the results.
☐	**MONITOR** the BCS for anomalous *behavior.*
☐	If anomalous behavior is still evident, **REPEAT** the detection procedures and/or mitigation procedures as necessary.
☐	When the layer or sub-system is operating without evidence of the cyber incident, and the Recovery Procedures Coordinator gives approval, **RECONNECT** the isolated layer or sub-system to the BCS.
☐	**MONITOR** the system for anomalous behavior.
☐	If anomalous behavior is still evident, **REPEAT** the detection procedures and/or mitigation procedures as necessary.
☐	**SUBMIT** all records of recovery actions to the Recovery Procedures Coordinator.
☐	**RETURN** to *routine monitoring* of the network.

■ **Note**   Customize the form to suit your specific building. Verify the normal operating conditions when the recovery procedures are prepared.

BUILDING CONTROLS SYSTEM FIELD TEST

- All point-to-point testing of end field devices through proper input/output to graphic and operator interface shall be completed and approved.

- All field calibration shall be completed and approved.

- Detailed functional tests shall verify that the system adheres to the Sequence of Operation.

- All alarm limits shall be completed and approved.

- All schedule start/stops and system setpoints shall be entered, operating and approved.

General

Adjust, calibrate, measure, program, configure, set the time schedules, and ensure that the systems function as specified in the Sequence of Operations.

Systems Check

An item-by-item check shall be performed for each HVAC system.

Step 1: System Inspection: With the system in unoccupied mode and with fan hand-off-auto switches in the OFF position, it shall be verified that power and main air are available where required and that all output devices are in their failsafe and normal positions. Each local display panel and each M&C Client shall be inspected to verify that all displays indicate shutdown conditions.

Step 2: Calibration Accuracy Check: A two-point accuracy check of the calibration of each HVAC control system sensing element and transmitter shall be performed by comparing the value from the test instrument to the corresponding SNVT. Digital indicating test instruments shall be used, such as digital thermometers, motor-driven psychrometers, and tachometers. The test instruments shall be at least twice as accurate as the specified sensor accuracy. The calibration of the test instruments shall be traceable to National Institute of Standards and Technology standards. The first checkpoint shall be with the HVAC system in unoccupied mode with fan hand-off-auto switches in the OFF position, and the second check point shall be with the HVAC system in an operational condition. Calibration checks shall verify that the sensing element-to-DDC system readout accuracies at two points are within the specified product accuracy tolerances. If not, the device shall be recalibrated or replaced and the calibration check repeated.

Step 3: Actuator Range Check: With the system running, a signal shall be applied to each actuator through the DDC Hardware controller. Proper operation of the actuators and positioners for all actuated devices shall be verified and the signal levels shall be recorded for the extreme positions of each device. The signal shall be varied over its full range, and it shall be verified that the actuators travel from zero stroke to full stroke within the signal range. Where applicable, it shall be verified that all sequenced actuators move from zero stroke to full stroke in the proper direction, and move the connected device in the proper direction from one extreme position to the other.

BOILER OR PRESSURE VESSEL

Functional Performance Test

☐	Incident Response Team shall inspect, restart, and verify the proper operation of boilers, including the following (IRT to sign off each item):
☐	**OBSERVE** the burner flame to identify combustion problems.
☐	Before lighting a boiler, always **PURGE** the furnace thoroughly. This is particularly important if oil has spilled into the furnace. The purge will evacuate the inventory of unburned gases until the concentration is below the explosive limits.
☐	**VERIFY** that the water treatment system is operating properly, producing boiler feedwater for the temperatures and pressures involved.
☐	**NEVER**—under any circumstance—disable a low-water trip.
☐	**VERIFY** that the water leaving the deaerator is free of oxygen, that the deaerator is operated at the proper pressure, and that the storage tank water is at saturation temperature. A continuous vent from the deaerator is necessary to **DISCHARGE** non-condensable gases.
☐	Continuously **MONITOR** the quality of condensate coming back from the process to enable the diversion of the condensate in the event of a catastrophic process equipment failure.
☐	**NEVER** blowdown a furnace wall header while the boiler is operating.
☐	**ALWAYS** ensure that the steam drum vent valve is open whenever the boiler pressure is less than 5 psig.
☐	The boiler's warm-up curve should be strictly followed. The standard warm-up curve for a typical boiler is not to increase the boiler water temperature over 100°F per hour. It is not unusual for a continuous minimum fire to exceed this maximum warm-up rate. During start-up, the burner must be intermittently fired to **ENSURE** that this rate is not exceeded.
☐	If necessary, **DRAIN** and flush the boiler, open all handholes and manholes, clean and remove soot and scale from the firesides.
☐	**INSTALL** new gaskets, **REPLACE** all handhole and manhole covers, **REFILL** boiler and **PERFORM** a hydrostatic test, if required.
☐	**DISASSEMBLE** the low-water cutoff and water feeding devices. Clean, recondition, and reassemble them. Leak **TEST** all fuel safety-shutoff valves.

■ **Note** Fill out one form for each boiler.

CHILLED WATER SYSTEM
Functional Performance Test

Chiller No.: CH-1

Incident Response Team shall inspect, restart, and verify the proper operation of chillers, including the following (IRT to sign off each item):	
☐	**START** the building air handling units to provide a cooling load for the chiller.
☐	**SWITCH** system to "warm-up" mode to open all supply ducts where VAV boxes may be present. Set fan-powered box coils to full heat.
☐	**OPERATE** boilers or use outside air to provide cooling load in the building, depending upon the outside air temperature and the design conditions to be simulated.

RECORD chiller inlet/outlet pressure readings and compare to chiller design conditions, Test and Balance Report, and chiller manufacturer's performance data.

	Chilled water flow			gpm
	DESIGN	**TEST & BAL**	**FULL PERF TEST**	**ACTUAL**
Chiller Inlet Pressure (psig)				
Chiller Outlet Pressure (psig)				

RECORD chilled water supply, return temperature readings, and compare to readout on chiller control panel.

	DISPLAYED	ACTUAL
Chilled Water Supply Temp (°F)		
Chilled Water Return Temp (°F)		

RECORD for chiller: amperage each phase, voltage phase to phase, voltage phase to ground, and power factor

	PHASE 1		PHASE 2		PHASE 3
Amperage					
Voltage					
Voltage					
Voltage to Ground					
Power Factor					
KW (use PMT)					

RECORD for chilled water pump: amperage each phase, voltage phase to phase, voltage phase to ground, and power factor.

	PHASE 1		PHASE 2		PHASE 3
Amperage					
Voltage					
Voltage					
Voltage to Ground					
Power Factor					
KW (use PMT)					

RECORD the following information:

Ambient outside air DB temperature (°F):	
Entering chilled water temperature (°F):	
Leaving chilled water temperature (°F):	

■ **Note**   Customize the form to suit your specific building. Verify the normal operating conditions when the recovery procedures are prepared. Confirm the energy performance over load range. The chiller should run one hour before performing load tests.

AIR HANDLING UNIT
Functional Performance Test

AIR HANDLER No.: AHU-1

Incident Response Team shall inspect, restart, and verify the proper operation of air handling unit, including the following (IRT to sign off each item):	
☐	**ENSURE** a slight negative pressure exists on inboard side of outside air dampers throughout the operation of the dampers. **MODULATE** OA, RA, and EA dampers from fully open to fully closed positions.
The following shall be **VERIFIED**. Supply and return fans (where applicable) operating mode is initiated:	
☐	(1) All dampers in **NORMAL** position prior to fan start.
☐	(2) All valves in **NORMAL** position prior to fan start.
☐	(3) System safeties allow start if safety conditions are met.
☐	(4) VAV fan controller shall **SOFT-START** fan.
☐	(5) **MODULATE** all VAV boxes to minimum airflow and verify that the static pressure does not exceed the high static pressure shutdown setpoint.
☐	(6) Return all VAV boxes to **AUTO**.
Occupied mode of operation: economizer de-energized.	
☐	(1) Outside air damper is at **MINIMUM** position.
☐	(2) Return air damper is **OPEN**.
☐	(3) Relief air damper is at **MINIMUM** position.
☐	(4) Chilled water control valve **MODULATING** to maintain leaving air temperature setpoint.

SETPOINT		deg F.	Actual		deg F.

☐	Fan VAV controller receiving signal from duct static pressure sensor and **MODULATING** fan to maintain supply duct static pressure setpoint.

SETPOINT		inches-wg	Actual		inches-wg

Occupied mode of operation—economizer energized.				
☐	(1) Outside air damper **MODULATED** to maintain mixed air temperature setpoint.			
SETPOINT		deg F.	**Actual**	deg F.
Outside air damper position			percent	
☐	(2) Relief air damper **MODULATES** with outside air damper per sequence of operation.			
Relief air damper position			percent	
☐	**(3) Chilled water control valve MODULATING to maintain leaving air temperature setpoint.**			
SETPOINT		deg F.	**Actual**	deg F.
☐	**(4) Hot-water control valve MODULATING to maintain leaving air temperature setpoint.**			
SETPOINT		deg F.	**Actual**	deg F.
☐	(5) Fan VAV controller receives signal from duct static pressure sensor and **MODULATES** fan to maintain supply duct static pressure setpoint.			
SETPOINT		inches-wg	**Actual**	inches-wg
Unoccupied mode of operation.				
☐	(1) **OBSERVE** fan starts when space temperature calls for heating or cooling.			
Note: This does not apply to series boxes.				
☐	(2) All dampers in **NORMAL** position.			
☐	(3) **VERIFY** space temp is maintained as specified in sequence of operation.			
The following shall be **VERIFIED** when the supply and return fans (where applicable) off mode is initiated:				
☐	(1) All dampers in **NORMAL** position.			
☐	(2) All valves in **NORMAL** position.			
☐	(3) Fan **DE-ENERGIZES**.			

VERIFY the chilled water coil control valve operation by setting all VAVs to maximum and minimum cooling.			
Max Cooling Supply air temp:		deg F,	**VERIFY** cooling valve operation
Min Cooling Supply air temp:		deg F,	**VERIFY** cooling valve operation
☐	**VERIFY** safety shut down initiated by low-temperature protection thermostat.		
☐	**VERIFY** that occupancy schedule is programmed into time clock/UMCS.		

■ **Note**   Customize the form to suit your specific building. Verify the normal operating conditions when the recovery procedures are prepared.

COMPUTER ROOM AIR CONDITIONER

Functional Performance Test

CRAC No.: CR-1

	Incident Response Team shall inspect, restart, and verify the proper operation of computer room unit in accordance with specification, including the following (IRT to sign off each item):
☐	System safeties allow start if safety conditions are met.
☐	**VERIFY** cooling and heating operation by varying thermostat setpoint from space setpoint to space setpoint plus 10 degrees, space setpoint minus 10 degrees, and returning to space setpoint.
☐	**VERIFY** humidifier operation by varying humidistat setpoint from space setpoint to space setpoint plus 20 percent RH, and returning to space setpoint.
☐	**VERIFY** that airflow is within tolerance.

■ **Note**   Customize the form to suit your specific building. Verify the normal operating conditions when the recovery procedures are prepared. Fill out one form for each CRAC unit.

COOLING TOWER
Functional Performance Test

Cooling Tower No.: CT-1

Incident Response Team shall inspect, restart, and verify the proper operation of cooling towers, including the following (IRT to sign off each item):	
☐	**START** the building air handling units to provide a cooling load.
☐	**SWITCH** system to "warm-up" mode to open all supply ducts, where VAV boxes may be present. Set fan-powered box coils to full heat.
☐	**OPERATE** boilers or use outside air to provide cooling load in building, depending upon the outside air temperature and the design conditions to be simulated.

RECORD CWS Header and CWR Header temperature readings and compare to cooling tower design conditions, Test and Balance Report, and manufacturer's performance data.

Water Flow Rate		gpm

RECORD the cooling tower water supply and return temperature readings. Compare to readout on the cooling tower control panel.

	DISPLAYED	ACTUAL
Cooling Water Supply Header Temp (°F)		
Cooling Water Return Header Temp (°F)		
Entering Wet Bulb Temp (°F)		

■ **Note**   Customize the form to suit your specific building. Verify the normal operating conditions when the recovery procedures are prepared.

Ambient Air Conditions	
Dry Bulb (°F)	
Wet Bulb (°F)	
Relative Humidity (%)	
Conditions at Cooling Tower Exit	
Dry Bulb (°F)	
Wet Bulb (°F)	
Relative Humidity (%)	

PUMP: PRIMARY CHILLED WATER

Functional Performance Test

Pump No.: PCHW-1

IRT shall demonstrate operation of pumps in accordance with specifications, including the following: **ACTIVATE** pump start using control system commands.					
☐	**VERIFY** correct operation in:				
HAND	☐	**OFF**	☐	**AUTO**	☐
☐	**VERIFY** pressure drop across strainer:				
		Strainer inlet pressure		psig	
		Strainer outlet pressure		psig	
☐	**VERIFY** pump inlet/outlet pressure reading, compare to Testing, Adjusting, and Balancing (TAB) Report and pump design conditions.				
	DESIGN		**TAB**		**ACTUAL**
Pump inlet pressure psig					
Pump outlet pressure psig					
☐	**OPERATE** pump at shutoff and at 100 percent of designed flow when all components are in full flow. **PLOT** test readings on pump curve and compare results against readings taken from flow measuring devices.				
		SHUTOFF		**100 PERCENT**	
	Pump inlet pressure psig				
	Pump outlet pressure psig				
	Pump flow rate gpm				
			SETPOINT		
	Differential Pressure Transmitter				
☐	For variable speed pumps, **OPERATE** pump at shutoff (shutoff to be done in manual on variable speed drive at the minimum rpm that the system is being controlled at) and at minimum flow or when all components are in full bypass. **PLOT** test readings on pump curve and compare results against readings taken from flow measuring devices.				

		SHUTOFF		100 PERCENT	
	Pump inlet pressure psig				
	Pump outlet pressure psig				
	Pump flow rate gpm				
			SETPOINT		
	Differential Pressure Transmitter				

MEASURE motor amperage each phase and voltage phase to phase and phase to ground for both the full flow and the minimum flow conditions. **COMPARE** amperage to nameplate FLA.					
Full flow:					
Nameplate FLA					
Amperage Phase 1		Phase 2		Phase 3	
Voltage Ph1-Ph2		Ph1-Ph3		Ph2-Ph3	
Voltage Ph1-gnd		Ph2-gnd		Ph3-gnd	
Minimum flow:					
Amperage Phase 1		Phase 2		Phase 3	
Voltage Ph1-Ph2		Ph1-Ph3		Ph2-Ph3	
Voltage Ph1-gnd		Ph2-gnd		Ph3-gnd	
Note any unusual noise.					

■ **Note** Customize the form to suit your specific building. Verify the normal operating conditions when the recovery procedures are prepared.

PUMP: SECONDARY CHILLED WATER

Functional Performance Test

Pump No.: SCHW-1

IRT shall demonstrate the operation of pumps in accordance with specifications, including the following: **ACTIVATE** pump start using control system commands.

☐	**VERIFY** correct operation in:					
HAND	☐	**OFF**	☐	**AUTO**	☐

☐	**VERIFY** pressure drop across strainer:		
		Strainer inlet pressure		psig
		Strainer outlet pressure		psig

☐	**VERIFY** pump inlet/outlet pressure reading, compare to Testing, Adjusting, and Balancing (TAB) Report and pump design conditions.				
	DESIGN		**TAB**		**ACTUAL**
Pump inlet pressure psig					
Pump outlet pressure psig					

☐	**OPERATE** pump at shutoff and at 100 percent of designed flow when all components are in full flow. **PLOT** test readings on pump curve and compare results against readings taken from flow measuring devices.			
		SHUTOFF		**100 PERCENT**
	Pump inlet pressure psig			
	Pump outlet pressure psig			
	Pump flow rate gpm			
		SETPOINT		
	Differential Pressure Transmitter			

☐	For variable speed pumps, **OPERATE** pump at shutoff (shutoff to be done in manual on variable speed drive at the minimum rpm that the system is being controlled at) and at minimum flow or when all components are in full bypass. **PLOT** test readings on pump curve and compare results against readings taken from flow measuring devices.

		SHUTOFF		100 PERCENT	
	Pump inlet pressure psig				
	Pump outlet pressure psig				
	Pump flow rate gpm				
			SETPOINT		
	Differential Pressure Transmitter				

■ **Note** Customize the form to suit your specific building. Verify the normal operating conditions when the recovery procedures are prepared.

MEASURE motor amperage each phase and voltage phase to phase and phase to ground for both the full flow and the minimum flow conditions. **COMPARE** amperage to nameplate FLA.					
Full flow:					
Nameplate FLA					
Amperage Phase 1		Phase 2		Phase 3	
Voltage Ph1-Ph2		Ph1-Ph3		Ph2-Ph3	
Voltage Ph1-gnd		Ph2-gnd		Ph3-gnd	
Minimum flow:					
Amperage Phase 1		Phase 2		Phase 3	
Voltage Ph1-Ph2		Ph1-Ph3		Ph2-Ph3	
Voltage Ph1-gnd		Ph2-gnd		Ph3-gnd	
Note any unusual noise.					

■ **Note** Customize the form to suit your specific building. Verify the normal operating conditions when the recovery procedures are prepared.

PUMP: PRIMARY DOMESTIC HOT WATER

Functional Performance Test

IRT shall demonstrate operation of pumps in accordance with specifications, including the following: **ACTIVATE** pump start using control system commands.					
☐	**VERIFY** correct operation in:				
HAND	☐	OFF	☐	AUTO	☐
☐	**VERIFY** pressure drop across strainer:				
		Strainer inlet pressure		psig	
		Strainer outlet pressure		psig	
☐	**VERIFY** pump inlet/outlet pressure reading, compare to Testing, Adjusting, and Balancing (TAB) Report and pump design conditions.				

	DESIGN		TAB		ACTUAL
Pump inlet pressure psig					
Pump outlet pressure psig					

☐	**OPERATE** pump at shutoff and at 100 percent of designed flow when all components are in full flow. **PLOT** test readings on pump curve and compare results against readings taken from flow measuring devices.		

		SHUTOFF		100 PERCENT	
	Pump inlet pressure psig				
	Pump outlet pressure psig				
	Pump flow rate gpm				
		SETPOINT			
	Differential Pressure Transmitter				

☐	For variable speed pumps, **OPERATE** pump at shutoff (shutoff to be done in manual on variable speed drive at the minimum rpm that the system is being controlled at) and at minimum flow or when all components are in full bypass. **PLOT** test readings on pump curve and compare results against readings taken from flow measuring devices.

		SHUTOFF		100 PERCENT	
	Pump inlet pressure psig				
	Pump outlet pressure psig				
	Pump flow rate gpm				
			SETPOINT		
	Differential Pressure Transmitter				

MEASURE motor amperage each phase and voltage phase to phase and phase to ground for both the full flow and the minimum flow conditions. **COMPARE** amperage to nameplate FLA.					
Full flow:					
Nameplate FLA					
Amperage Phase 1		Phase 2		Phase 3	
Voltage Ph1-Ph2		Ph1-Ph3		Ph2-Ph3	
Voltage Ph1-gnd		Ph2-gnd		Ph3-gnd	
Minimum flow:					
Amperage Phase 1		Phase 2		Phase 3	
Voltage Ph1-Ph2		Ph1-Ph3		Ph2-Ph3	
Voltage Ph1-gnd		Ph2-gnd		Ph3-gnd	
Note any unusual noise.					

■ **Note**   Customize the form to suit your specific building. Verify the normal operating conditions when the recovery procedures are prepared.

PUMP: SECONDARY DOMESTIC HOT WATER

Functional Performance Test

Pump No.: SDHW-1

IRT shall demonstrate the operation of pumps in accordance with specifications, including the following: **ACTIVATE** pump start using control system commands.							
☐	**VERIFY** correct operation in:						
HAND	☐		**OFF**	☐		**AUTO**	☒
☐	**VERIFY** pressure drop across strainer:						
			Strainer inlet pressure			psig	
			Strainer outlet pressure			psig	
☐	**VERIFY** pump inlet/outlet pressure reading, compare to Testing, Adjusting, and Balancing (TAB) Report and pump design conditions.						
	DESIGN		**TAB**			**ACTUAL**	
Pump inlet pressure psig							
Pump outlet pressure psig							
☐	**OPERATE** pump at shutoff and at 100 percent of designed flow when all components are in full flow. **PLOT** test readings on pump curve and compare results against readings taken from flow measuring devices.						
		SHUTOFF		**100 PERCENT**			
	Pump inlet pressure psig						
	Pump outlet pressure psig						
	Pump flow rate gpm						
		SETPOINT					
	Differential Pressure Transmitter						
☐	For variable speed pumps, **OPERATE** pump at shutoff (shutoff to be done in manual on variable speed drive at the minimum rpm that the system is being controlled at) and at minimum flow or when all components are in full bypass. **PLOT** test readings on pump curve and compare results against readings taken from flow measuring devices.						

		SHUTOFF			100 PERCENT	
	Pump inlet pressure psig					
	Pump outlet pressure psig					
	Pump flow rate gpm					
			SETPOINT			
	Differential Pressure Transmitter					

MEASURE motor amperage each phase and voltage phase to phase and phase to ground for both the full flow and the minimum flow conditions. **COMPARE** amperage to nameplate FLA.

Full flow:

Nameplate FLA					
Amperage Phase 1		Phase 2		Phase 3	
Voltage Ph1-Ph2		Ph1-Ph3		Ph2-Ph3	
Voltage Ph1-gnd		Ph2-gnd		Ph3-gnd	

Minimum flow:

Amperage Phase 1		Phase 2		Phase 3	
Voltage Ph1-Ph2		Ph1-Ph3		Ph2-Ph3	
Voltage Ph1-gnd		Ph2-gnd		Ph3-gnd	

Note any unusual noise.

■ **Note** Customize the form for your specific building. Verify the normal operating conditions when the recovery procedures are prepared.

FAN COIL UNIT

Functional Performance Test

Fan Coil Unit No.: FCU - 1

IRT shall demonstrate operation of selected fan coils in accordance with specifications, including the following:				
☐	Cooling only fan coils: **VERIFY** fan coil unit response to room temp setpoint adjustment.			
		CHECK blower fan airflow		cfm
		CHECK cooling coil water flow		gpm
☐	**VERIFY** proper operation of cooling water control valve.			
☐	**CHECK** cooling mode inlet air temperature			deg F
☐	**CHECK** cooling mode outlet air temperature			deg F
☐	**MEASURE** coil sensible capacity and compare to design:			
	ACTUAL		BTU/hr	DESIGN	BTU/hr
☐	Cooling/heating fan coils: **VERIFY** fan coil unit response to room temp setpoint adjustment			
☐	**CHECK** blower fan airflow.			cfm
☐	**CHECK** cooling coil water flow.			gpm
☐	**VERIFY** proper operation of cooling water control valve.			
☐	**CHECK** cooling mode inlet air temperature.			deg F
☐	**CHECK** cooling mode outlet air temperature.			deg F
☐	**MEASURE** cooling coil sensible capacity and compare to design:			
	ACTUAL		BTU/hr	DESIGN	BTU/hr
☐	**CHECK** heating coil water flow.			gpm
☐	**VERIFY** proper operation of heating water control valve.			
☐	**CHECK** heating mode inlet air temperature.			deg F
☐	**CHECK** heating mode outlet air temperature.			deg F
☐	**MEASURE** heating coil capacity and compare to design:			
	ACTUAL		BTU/hr	DESIGN	BTU/hr

■ **Note**   Customize the form to suit your specific building. Verify the normal operating conditions when the recovery procedures are prepared. Fill out one form for each fan coil unit.

DIESEL BACKUP GENERATOR

Functional Performance Test

Generator No.: DG-1

	IRT shall demonstrate the operation of backup generators in accordance with specifications, including the following: **START** equipment to provide energy source for building recovery.				
☐	**VERIFY** that backup generators are providing recoverable energy.				
☐	**VERIFY** that recovery system senses available energy and activates.				
		DESIGN		**ACTUAL**	
	Primary inlet air temp		deg F		deg F
	Primary outlet air temp		deg F		deg F
	Primary flow rate		cfm		cfm
	Secondary inlet air temp		deg F		deg F
	Secondary outlet air temp		deg F		deg F
	Secondary flow rate		cfm		cfm
	Primary energy BTU/hr		BTU/hr		BTU/hr
	Secondary energy BTU/hr		BTU/hr		BTU/hr
☐	**VERIFY** that the switchgear senses available energy and activates.				

■ **Note** Customize the form for your specific building and verify the normal operating conditions when the recovery procedures are prepared.

VENTILATION UNIT

Functional Performance Test

Ventilation System No.: V-1

Incident Response Team shall inspect, restart, and verify the proper operation of the air handling unit, including the following (IRT to sign off each item):	
☐	**ENSURE** that a slight negative pressure exists on the inboard side of outside air dampers throughout the operation of the dampers. **MODULATE** OA, RA, and EA dampers from fully open to fully closed positions.
The following shall be **VERIFIED**. Supply and return fans (where applicable) operating mode is initiated:	
☐	All dampers in **NORMAL** position prior to fan start.
☐	All valves in **NORMAL** position prior to fan start.
☐	System safeties allow start if safety conditions are met.
☐	VAV fan controller shall **SOFT-START** fan.
☐	**MODULATE** all VAV boxes to **MINIMUM** airflow and verify that the static pressure does not exceed the high static pressure shutdown setpoint.
	RETURN all VAV boxes to auto.

Occupied mode of operation—economizer **DE-ENERGIZED**.

☐	Outside air damper is at **MINIMUM** position.				
☐	Make sure that the return air damper is **OPEN**.				
☐	Relief air damper is at **MINIMUM** position.				
☐	Chilled water control valve is **MODULATING** to maintain leaving air temperature setpoint.				
	SETPOINT		deg F.	**ACTUAL**	deg F.
☐	Fan VAV controller receiving signal from duct static pressure sensor and **MODULATING** fan to **MAINTAIN** supply duct static pressure setpoint.				
	SETPOINT		inches-wg	**ACTUAL**	inches-wg

Occupied mode of operation— economizer **ENERGIZED**.

	Outside air damper **MODULATED** to maintain mixed air temperature setpoint.				
	SETPOINT		deg F.	**ACTUAL**	deg F.
☐	Outside air damper position			percent	
☐	Relief air damper **MODULATES** with outside air damper per sequence of operation.				
	Relief air damper position			percent	
☐	Chilled water control valve **MODULATING** to maintain leaving air temperature setpoint.				
	SETPOINT		deg F.	**ACTUAL**	deg F.
☐	Hot-water control valve **MODULATING** to maintain leaving air temperature setpoint.				
	SETPOINT		deg F.	**ACTUAL**	deg F.

	Fan VAV controller receives signal from duct static pressure sensor and modulates fan to **MAINTAIN** supply duct static pressure setpoint.				
	SETPOINT		inches-wg	**ACTUAL**		inches-wg
Unoccupied mode of operation					
☐	**OBSERVE** fan starts when space temperature calls for heating or cooling.				
Note: **This does not apply to series boxes.**					
☐	All dampers are in **NORMAL** position.				
☐	**VERIFY** space temp is maintained as specified in sequence of operation.				
☐	The following shall be verified when the supply and return fans (where applicable) **OFF MODE** is initiated:				
☐	All dampers are in **NORMAL** position.				
☐	All valves are in **NORMAL** position.				
☐	Fan **DE-ENERGIZES**.				
☐	**VERIFY** the chilled water coil control valve operation by setting all VAV's to maximum and minimum cooling.				
	Max Cooling Supply air temp:			deg F, Verify cooling valve operation	
	Min Cooling Supply air temp:			deg F, Verify cooling valve operation	
☐	**VERIFY** safety shut down initiated by low temperature protection thermostat.				
☐	**VERIFY** occupancy schedule is programmed into time clock/UMCS.				

■ **Note** Customize the form to suit your specific building and verify the normal operating conditions when the recovery procedures are prepared.

ELECTRICAL SWITCHGEAR CHECKLIST

Functional Performance Test

Switchgear No.: S-1

Incident Response Team shall inspect, restart, and verify the proper operation of electrical switchgear, including the following (IRT to sign off each item):	
	CHECK for voltage imbalance. Maximum allowable is 2%.

Insulation Resistance Test

☐	**INSPECT** to make sure that surface dust and moisture have been removed from the component under test.
☐	**ENSURE** that the component is isolated from other connected systems, which may feed back to other components or circuits not under test.
☐	Voltage shall be **applied** between one phase and other phases connected with ground; testing shall be repeated for other phases.
☐	The following shall be verified when the supply and return fans' (where applicable) **OFF MODE** is initiated:

High Voltage Test

☐	**DETERMINE** that the equipment is in proper condition to put back in service by performing the following tests:
☐	AC Hi-pot test for switchgear with leakage current indicator for overload protection.
☐	DC Hi-pot test for cables with leakage current indicator for overload protection.

INTEGRATED SYSTEMS TEST: EMERGENCY POWER

Building:		Date:	
Participants			
Individual Name:		**Participation Role:**	
Date of Test		**Weather**	
Date of Test		**Weather**	
Date of Test		**Weather**	
Date of Test		**Weather**	
Testing Procedures and Record			
Sequence of Operation	**Pass**	**Fail**	**Comments**
Example: Duct static maintained at setpoint.	☐	☒	Fire smoke damper is closed and needs to be open to provide air to the duct static sensor.
	☐	☐	
	☐	☐	
	☐	☐	
	☐	☐	

INTEGRATED SYSTEMS TEST: EMERGENCY POWER

Testing Procedures and Record			
Sequence of Operation	**Pass**	**Fail**	**Comments**
Chilled Water System			
Upon power failure, **VERIFY** that the following occurs:			
Chillers **SHUT DOWN**. After transfer of power, chillers **RESTART**.	☐	☐	
VERIFY that chillers return to previous operation.	☐	☐	
Pumps **MAINTAIN** operation. After transfer of power via open transition, pumps **RESTART**.	☐	☐	
VERIFY that pumps return to previous operation.	☐	☐	
Load is **MAINTAINED**.	☐	☐	
Temperatures **REMAIN** within operational range.	☐	☐	
CHW Flows **REMAIN** within operational range.	☐	☐	
Loss of power alarms are **TRIGGERED** at BCS for chillers and pumps.	☐	☐	
Condenser Water System			
Upon power failure, **VERIFY** that the following occurs:			
Cooling Towers **MAINTAIN** operation. After transfer of power via open transition, cooling towers **RESTART**.	☐	☐	
VERIFY cooling towers return to previous operation.	☐	☐	
Pumps **MAINTAIN** operation. After transfer of power via open transition, pumps **RESTART**.	☐	☐	
VERIFY that pumps return to previous operation.	☐	☐	
Load is **MAINTAINED**.	☐	☐	
Temperatures **REMAIN** within operational range.	☐	☐	
CW Flows **REMAIN** within operational range.	☐	☐	

INTEGRATED SYSTEMS TEST: EMERGENCY POWER

Testing Procedures and Record			
Sequence of Operation	**Pass**	**Fail**	**Comments**
Loss of power alarms are **TRIGGERED** at BCS for cooling towers and pumps.	☐	☐	
Heating Water System			
Upon power failure, **VERIFY** that the following occurs:			
Boilers **MAINTAIN** operation. After transfer of power via open transition, cooling towers **RESTART**.	☐	☐	
VERIFY that boilers return to previous operation.	☐	☐	
Pumps **MAINTAIN** operation. After transfer of power via open transition, pumps **RESTART**.	☐	☐	
VERIFY that pumps return to previous operation.	☐	☐	
Load is **MAINTAINED**.	☐	☐	
Temperatures **REMAIN** within operational range.	☐	☐	
CW Flows **REMAIN** within operational range.	☐	☐	
Loss of power alarms are **TRIGGERED** at BCS for boilers and pumps.	☐	☐	

OPERATIONAL SECURITY LOG

Date: Time	Asset	Operator: IP Address	Description	Action Taken	Results

HVAC CONTROL SYSTEM DRAWINGS

The Design Drawing Legend indicates all symbols, abbreviations, and acronyms.

VALVE SCHEDULE

The valve schedule indicates each valve's size, flow coefficient Kv (Cv), pressure drop at specified flow rate, spring range, positive positioner range, actuator size, close off pressure to torque data, dimensions, and access and clearance requirements data. The valve schedule contains actuator data of the force required to move and seal the valve.

Valve Schedule							
ID No	Size	Flow Kv	Pres Drop	Spring Rng	Pos Rng	Torq	Dim. & Clear

Comments:

DAMPER SCHEDULE

The damper schedule indicates each damper's unique identifier, type (opposed or parallel blade), nominal and actual sizes, orientation of axis and frame, direction of blade rotation, actuator size and spring ranges, operation rate, positive positioner range, location of actuators and damper end switches, arrangement of sections in multi-section dampers, and methods of connecting dampers, actuators, and linkages. The Damper Schedule indicates the AMCA 511 maximum leakage rate at the operating static-pressure differential.

Damper Schedule	
ID No.	Location

THERMOSTAT AND OCCUPANCY SENSOR SCHEDULE

The thermostat and occupancy sensor schedule indicate each area's unique room identifier and control features and functions.

Thermostat and Occupancy Sensor Schedule	
ID No.	Location

BUILDING EQUIPMENT SCHEDULE

The equipment schedule indicates the unique identifier, manufacturer, model number, part number, and descriptive name for each control device, hardware, and component installed.

Equipment Schedule				
ID No	Descriptive Name	Manufacturer	Model Number	Part Number
	Boiler			
	Chiller			
	Cooling Tower			
	Water Heater			
	Air Handling Unit			
	Pressure Vessel			
	Primary CW Pump			
	Second CW Pump			
	Primary HW Pump			
	Second HW Pump			
	Generator			

BUILDING OCCUPANCY SCHEDULE

The occupancy schedule indicates the seasonal building start time for building equipment to reach the required building temperature and the time that equipment is set back to caretaker temperature.

Occupancy Schedule			
	HVAC Start/Stop Times	Office Lighting Times	Comments
Spring			
Sun			unoccupied
Mon	0530–2200	0600–2200	74 deg F. 15% to 55% humidity
Tues	0530–2200	0600–2200	74 deg F. 15% to 55% humidity
Wed	0530–2200	0600–2200	74 deg F. 15% to 55% humidity
Thurs	0530–2200	0600–2200	74 deg F. 15% to 55% humidity
Fri	0530–2000	0600–2000	74 deg F. 15% to 55% humidity
Sat			unoccupied
Summer			
Sun			
Mon			
Tues			
Wed			
Thurs			
Fri			
Sat			

(*continued*)

Occupancy Schedule			
	HVAC Start/Stop Times	Office Lighting Times	Comments
Fall			
Sun			
Mon			
Tues			
Wed			
Thurs			
Fri			
Sat			
Winter			
Sun			
Mon			
Tues			
Wed			
Thurs			
Fri			
Sat			

POINTS SCHEDULE

The Points Schedule drawing indicates the Device address and NodeID, Input and Output SNVTs, including SNVT Name, Type and Description, Hardware I/O, including Type (AI, AO, BI, BO) and Description.

Points Schedule	

BUILDING CONTROL NETWORK RISER DIAGRAM

The Riser Diagram for all DDC hardware and network hardware, including network terminators, shall be attached. It provides the unique identifier, common descriptive name, physical sequential order (previous and next device on the network), room identifier, and location within a room.

SEQUENCE OF OPERATION

The Sequence of Operation is unique to each building and should be readily available to the IRT. These can be found in the as-built drawings, original project specifications, or manufacturer operating manuals. Attach a copy here.

Sequence of Operation	
Attached	**Operating and Maintenance Manuals**
☐	Boilers
☐	Chillers
☐	Cooling Towers
☐	Domestic Hot-Water Heaters
☐	Air Handling Units
☐	Pressure Vessels
☐	Primary Chilled-Water Pumps
☐	Secondary Chilled-Water Pumps
☐	Primary Domestic Hot-Water Pumps
☐	Secondary Domestic Hot-Water Pumps
☐	
☐	
☐	
☐	
☐	
☐	

PERFORMANCE VERIFICATION TEST RESULTS

The Performance Verification Test is unique to each building and should be readily available to the IRT.

Performance Verification Test Results	
Attached	**Description**
☐	
☐	
☐	
☐	
☐	
☐	
☐	
☐	
☐	
☐	
☐	
☐	
☐	
☐	
☐	
☐	
☐	

COMMISSIONING REPORT

The Commissioning Report is unique to each building and should be readily available to the IRT. The report includes checklists and functional test results that provide historical data that will be helpful for before and after comparison by the IRT.

EQUIPMENT MAINTENANCE MANUALS

All equipment manufacturers supply operating manuals with their equipment. Unfortunately, many buildings do not have manuals and operating instructions available. These manuals may have either been lost or misplaced. It is the responsibility of the supervisor to obtain these publications and see that they are read, understood, and followed, and that a hard copy is available in the Building Operations Center. Collect all manuals in one location.

Equipment Manuals	
Available	**Operating and Maintenance Manuals**
☐	Boilers
☐	Chillers
☐	Cooling Towers
☐	Domestic Hot-Water Heaters
☐	Air Handling Units
☐	Pressure Vessels
☐	Primary Chilled-Water Pumps
☐	Secondary Chilled-Water Pumps
☐	Primary Domestic Hot-Water Pumps
☐	Secondary Domestic Hot-Water Pumps
☐	
☐	
☐	
☐	

LIST OF AUTHORIZED MAINTENANCE LAPTOPS

The Authorized Maintenance Laptop List may be unique to each building and should be readily available to the IRT. The list includes the date of the last virus scan for each. Authorized maintenance laptops *must* be stored in a secure location and only issued to vendors on site for use on site. When needed for more than one day, laptops shall be collected at the end of each day and locked away. Laptops shall always be scanned for viruses and malware prior to connection to the BCS. After use, vendor software shall be wiped and the drive scanned prior to returning to storage.

Authorized Maintenance Laptop List	
Date of Last Virus Scan	**Laptop Number**

VENDOR CONTACT LIST

This is a listing of all vendors and contractors that currently provide support or will provide support in a post-disaster environment. Additionally, any service level agreements (SLAs) that have been executed and all subsequent modifications should be attached.

Vendor Contact List				
Vendor	Equipment	Contact Name	Telephone	Email

Index

© Luis Ayala 2016
L. Ayala, *Cyber-Physical Attack Recovery Procedures*, DOI 10.1007/978-1-4842-2065-8

Printed in the United States
By Bookmasters